ROCKIN' THE BOAT

ROCKIN' THE BOAT

50 Iconic Revolutionaries

FROM JOAN OF ARC TO MALCOLM X

JEFF FLEISCHER

Z

Zest Books
San Francisco

TABLE OF CONTENTS

ZEST BOOKS

Connect with Zest!

- zestbooks.net/blog
- zestbooks.net/contests
- twitter.com/zestbooks

- facebook.com/zestbook
- facebook.com/BooksWithATwist
- pinterest.com/zestbooks

35 Stillman Street, Suite 121, San Francisco, CA 94107 / www.zestbooks.net

Manufactured in the U.S.A.
DOC 10 9 8 7 6 5 4 3 2 1
4500514208

INTRODUCTION

As a kid without daily access to the Internet or cable, I first learned about a lot of important news stories on network TV—which meant that the story was important enough for each network to interrupt whatever it had been showing before. I remember watching TV one weekend when our regularly scheduled broadcast was set aside to show footage of Nelson Mandela, the South African revolutionary who had been in prison more than twice as long as I'd even been alive, walking out a free man. I'd learned about Mandela's struggle against South African apartheid in school, in magazines, even in music. I'd grown to admire him long before his release from prison, and I got to follow how his story changed history from there, right up until his death (just a few months before I began work on this book). Even to a kid, Mandela showed in real time how obviously one man could change the course of history for the better.

Not all the people in this book are as admirable as Mandela, but they were all important revolutionaries in their own time. Every one of them managed to gather a big enough following to go down in history. Some tried to overthrow governments or stop invasions, while others fought for the rights of minorities or the poor.

As you probably guessed, getting the list down to just fifty revolutionaries wasn't an easy task. The world's first dominant empire, that of the Assyrians, was fighting uprisings more than 4,000 years ago, so there's plenty of revolutionary history to choose from.

The list got narrowed a few ways. First, while it's perfectly fair to call somebody a revolutionary in just about any field, everybody here made their biggest impact by influencing (or trying to influence) who was in charge of their homeland or how those in charge treated their people. (That means no Albert Einstein or Bob Dylan or Leonardo da Vinci.) Second, lots of revolutions throughout history didn't have an obvious, clear-cut leader, and there were lots of revolutionary leaders about whom we either know little, or little that is true. Third, some figures didn't make the cut simply because their stories were similar to those of others on the list, and there was only so much room. If your favorite revolutionary isn't in the book, there's a good chance he or she was under serious consideration.

To be clear, this book isn't an attempt to put together a "top fifty" list or any kind of ranking. The fifty famous figures appear in the order of their birth, and each chapter gives a brief history of their life and accomplishments, along with some bonus facts. You can read them in order, skip around, or read some now and more later—it's up to you.

Part of the fun of putting the book together was getting a chance to revisit all these stories (as you might guess, I was a bit of a history nerd since childhood), reading through anything from college class notes to encyclopedias, rereading books like Livy's history of the Punic Wars or Nat Turner's dictated autobiography. I also got to search news articles to find material for sidebars, as a way to show how long-dead people still make history, from President Obama endorsing a holiday for Cesar Chavez to the New Zealand government still trying to address Hone Heke's concerns. Of course, whole books could be written about any one of these fifty—and they have. I hope this book makes you keen to learn more about at least a few revolutionaries, and definitely recommend using it as a springboard to read (or at least Google) more about anyone you find interesting. (You can find suggestions for related reading materials, along with updates about relevant historical discoveries, at http://zestbooks.net/rockin-the-boat.)

The people chosen for the final fifty were also selected for variety. Some are obviously "good guys" (it's hard to find much fault with Gandhi, for example). Others are pretty villainous, but most fit somewhere in between. For a lot of them, it really depends on which side is telling the story—as the old cliché goes, one person's freedom fighter is another's terrorist. Some of them emerged from their revolutions as big winners, others died in the service of a winning cause, and still others lost disastrously.

The final fifty span history, from Hannibal's stand against ancient Rome to the civil rights struggles of just a generation ago. They span the globe, representing every continent except Antarctica (counting Oceania instead of just Australia). Some became revolutionaries as teenagers, others late in life. They include slaves and generals, suffragettes and queens, Communists and nationalists.

What all fifty fascinating figures have in common is that each one—from Vercingetorix to Joan of Arc to Vladimir Lenin—started out as a huge underdog, but inspired supporters to fight for their cause. As John Lennon (no relation) and the Beatles put it in their song "Revolution," we all want to change the world. Win or lose, each of these fifty people can say they did. •

Hannibal Barca riding high on his war elephant at the battle of Zama. (Spoiler alert: not Hannibal's finest hour.)

HANNIBAL BARCA

THE TIME: *247–c. 183 BCE*

THE PLACE: *Carthage*

THE OPPONENT: *Rome*

I n its prime, Rome was the heavyweight champion of world empires, the kind you had to be lucky just to fight to a draw. To get there, though, Rome had to survive its toughest foe—the ingenious Carthaginian general Hannibal Barca.

Carthage, a Phoenician city-state on the North African coast of modern-day Tunisia, was the biggest rival Rome had, a naval and trade power that totally dominated the Mediterranean. The Romans and Carthaginians (who the Romans called Punics) were clearly *the* two regional superpowers by 264 BCE, when both sides were asked to intervene in a local war in Sicily. Things quickly got out of hand, and they soon wound up fighting each other in what became the thirteen-year-long First Punic War. After a series of Roman victories, Carthage agreed to a peace treaty, giving up its interest in Sicily (and several other territories) and agreeing to pay a hefty annual war debt to Rome.

It got worse. First, Rome waited until the Carthaginians started demilitarizing and then changed the terms of the peace, leaving Carthage no choice but to accept a larger debt. As a result, Carthage didn't have the money to pay its army—which mostly consisted of hired mercenaries from neighboring territories—and many of them angrily marched on the city. And while Carthage was busy fighting a full-scale war against its former mercenaries (using, naturally, more mercenaries), Rome grabbed control of a few under-defended Mediterranean islands.

None of this sat well with Hamilcar Barca, and he swore revenge for what the Romans had done. Probably the best of Carthage's military commanders, Hamilcar had personally gone undefeated in the Punic War. He felt betrayed

THE SINCEREST FORM OF FLATTERY

Hannibal's crossing of the Alps was such an impressive feat that future generals made a point of leading their own armies across the mountains. Julius Caesar, Charlemagne, and Napoleon Bonaparte all paid homage to Hannibal (and tried to show off) this way, but the Carthaginian general did it first—and with elephants.

when his government agreed to peace, and then got stuck having to fight against his own guys on its behalf. Once the ex-mercenaries were defeated, Hamilcar put together a new (also mostly mercenary) army and took it to Europe, where he spent the rest of his life conquering much of what's now Spain (Barcelona, for example, is named for his family).

While he was technically leading a Carthaginian army, Hamilcar was doing all this on his own authority, forging a military specifically loyal to him. Even by Carthaginian standards, he was no friend of Rome, and he made his oldest son, Hannibal, swear early in life that he would share that lifelong grudge. The boy definitely listened.

———

After Hamilcar drowned in battle against a Celtic tribe, and after the son-in-law who replaced him as commander was assassinated by a Celt, the army chose Hannibal—who'd grown up in the camp and fought alongside the men—as its new leader. Hannibal was only twenty-six at the time, but the government in Carthage went along with the decision.

Once in charge, Hannibal didn't waste much time keeping his promise to his father and rebelling against the harsh "peace" Rome had forced on Carthage. He immediately started conquering what was left of the Iberian Peninsula south of the Erbo River, a boundary set up by that treaty with Rome. He also exploited a technicality that gave him a clever excuse to start his planned revenge. The city of Saguntum had its own protection deal with Rome, but it was unfortunately located just south of that Erbo boundary. Claiming it was his right under the rules, in 219 Hannibal put the city under siege and, after a difficult battle, sacked it.

Hannibal, already a few moves ahead, watched his opponent move into position to give him exactly what he wanted. The Romans didn't risk actually helping the people of Saguntum by sending an army, but they did send ambassadors to Carthage to demand the government turn over Hannibal. He knew that wasn't going to happen, not when he was still following the letter of the treaty and had become a star back home for conquering so much territory. So, Rome declared war, and Hannibal instantly had a nice and legal excuse to go after his real target.

———

With the Roman navy in control of the Mediterranean and virtually no help coming from home, Hannibal had only one way to invade Italy. Depending on whose numbers are right, he had between 40,000 and 100,000 troops with him, plus nearly forty war elephants. His just-crazy-enough-to-work idea was to take that large, modern army across the Alps, a mission that seemed nearly impossible at the time.

Just getting his army through the Alps to Italy would have made Hannibal a legend, as they had to survive attacks from mountain tribes, deadly cold, limited supplies, and treacherous terrain that sent men and animals falling over the edge. Though Hannibal might have come out the other side with as few as 20,000 men and only a few elephants, the achievement proved he wasn't someone Rome could afford to take lightly.

He made sure the enemy knew it too, with a series of impressive victories against Roman legions on Italian soil. First at the river Trebia and then farther south at Lake Trasimene, Hannibal used the aggressiveness of Roman commanders against them, choosing the site and setting his battle formations the way he wanted before drawing the Roman armies into combat on his terms and completely annihilating them. Hannibal also worked to form alliances with the peoples of Italy, presenting himself as their best hope to be free of Roman rule—he even freed non-Roman soldiers taken prisoner after battles. Each victory made it easier to convince them that he had a real shot.

That got even easier after the Battle of Cannae, in which Hannibal again pulled off the seemingly impossible. By carefully deploying his battle formation and having the center of his army retreat slowly while the wings advanced, he was able to completely surround a force much larger than his own and hand it the worst defeat of the Second Punic War. The reported 70,000 deaths on the Roman side are probably an exaggeration, but whatever the number, it was definitely a lot. And it was not just how many died, but who died—including one of two current Roman consuls (basically co-presidents, elected every year), both the previous year's consuls, and a huge chunk of the Roman Senate and the ruling class.

Rome eventually figured out that its best hope was to go on offense against the Carthaginians anywhere they weren't commanded by this unbeatable general, and avoid facing Hannibal in battle as much as possible. While Hannibal and his army remained in Italy for a total of fifteen years, capturing cities and forming alliances, a Roman army successfully invaded Iberia. Hannibal's younger brother, Hasdrubal, who had been raising reinforcements for a potential attack on Rome itself, was killed in battle in Spain. Hannibal learned those reinforce-

A HARD ACT TO FOLLOW

Military commanders have long been obsessed with Hannibal's against-the-odds domination at Cannae. German strategist Alfred von Schlieffen called it "a perfect battle of annihilation" and used Cannae as the inspiration for his 1905 "Schlieffen Plan," a strategy for Germany to win a two-front war by encircling and defeating France and then turning to fight Russia. Germany gave this plan a try in World War I—and employed a version of it in World War II—only to find out just how difficult Hannibal's tactics were to imitate.

ments would not be coming when Roman riders approached his army and threw his brother's head into the camp.

Meanwhile, Rome's own rising-star general, Scipio, went to Africa. There, he formed an important alliance with the Numidians—Carthaginian neighbors whose cavalry had made up an important part of Hannibal's army—and prepared to attack Carthage itself. The government ordered Hannibal to come home and defend the city, so in 203 BCE he returned to Africa for the first time since he was a little boy. When treaty talks fell apart, Hannibal's forces met Scipio's at the Battle of Zama. Against a younger foe who had studied his tactics and learned how to use them against him, Hannibal suffered his first real defeat. Carthage soon agreed to an even harsher peace than before, one that cost a lot of money and all of its overseas territories, which made it a purely North African power, and gave Rome veto power over any Carthaginian military action, even within Africa.

After the war, when he was just forty-three, Hannibal ran for political office in Carthage, where he helped reform the city's government and rebuild its economy. His reforms worked so well that Carthage was again a prosperous city-state just seven years after Zama. Still seeing Hannibal as a threat, Rome demanded the Carthaginians turn him over, but he escaped. He spent the rest of his life in exile and on the run, serving as a military strategist for a series of Roman foes and fleeing capture over and over again. He was in his mid-sixties when the Romans eventually caught up to him in Bithynia, part of modern Turkey. With all the exits blocked and no escape in sight, Hannibal drank the poison he always carried in his ring for just such an occasion, rather than be taken alive.

Carthage itself suffered from a similar Roman obsession, despite a peace treaty that was supposed to protect it. In 149 BCE, after a series of intentionally unreasonable demands that tricked the Carthaginians into giving up weapons, hostages, and its navy, Rome broke the treaty and declared a Third Punic War with the sole intent of destroying Carthage. When the city fell in 146 after a brutal siege, Rome killed or enslaved the entire population, burned the city, and finally destroyed its most powerful rival for good. ●

JUDAH MACCABEE

THE TIME: *c. 190–160 BCE*

THE PLACE: *Judea*

THE OPPONENT: *The Seleucid Empire*

Started more than 5,000 years ago, Judaism is one of the oldest surviving religions in the world, and the Jewish people have spent nearly that long surviving threats from a long list of would-be conquerors. When the Seleucid Empire tried to force the people of Judea to give up their culture, Judah Maccabee led the fight to make sure that didn't happen.

When Judah was born in the second century BCE, the land of Judea was a small territory, just a fraction of modern Israel's size. The problem was its location had always placed it in the path of a series of regional powers, and the Babylonians, the Persians, and Alexander the Great's Macedonian Greeks took turns conquering Judea. When Alexander died unexpectedly in 332 BCE, his top generals divided up his empire and fought among themselves, and Judea changed hands again, this time falling under the rule of the Seleucid Empire (sometimes called the Syrian Greeks).

The empires that grew out of Alexander the Great's conquests all believed in "Hellenization," the practice of spreading Greek culture, language, and religion. The Seleucids were particularly harsh about it, and it only got worse under King Antiochus IV Epiphanes (the son of Antiochus the Great). In 167 BCE, Antiochus attacked and sacked the city of Jerusalem, which had previously been held by the less-extreme Ptolemaic Empire, and imposed Seleucid rule over Judea.

Antiochus flat-out banned the practice of Judaism, essentially trying to stop Jews from being Jewish, and ordering them to worship Zeus and other Greek gods. Obviously, this didn't sit well with the people, and many refused to comply. Antiochus sent an occupying army to enforce his laws, and tens of thousands of Jews were executed for disobeying.

Judah points toward victory in a nineteenth-century woodcut.

Others went along with the orders, and not just out of fear. In fact, a faction of Judeans supported Hellenization, and what became known as the Maccabean Revolt started in 167 as a civil war between those who wanted to assimilate and those who didn't.

———

The original revolutionary in the Maccabee family was Judah's father, Mattathias (sometimes known as Matisyahu), a prominent *cohen* who served as the religious leader for the town of Modi'in. He and his five sons—Simon, Eleazer, Judah, Jonanan, and Jonathan—fled Jerusalem and hid out in the forest after Mattathias killed a fellow Jew who made sacrifices to the Greek gods.

When Mattathias died in 166, Judah (though only the third-oldest son) took over leadership of the family and the supporters who joined the cause. Maccabee wasn't Judah's original surname; he picked up the name (which roughly translates as "the Hammer") during the rebellion, and the whole family became known by the fitting nickname.

The Maccabee brothers understood that guerilla tactics were their best chance at victory, and took the enemy by surprise whenever possible. Judah's first big victory came at Wadi Haramia, where his troops ambushed and defeated a larger Seleucid army and killed its commander. The win convinced more Jews who opposed Hellenization to join up, and Judah's forces produced another important victory at Emmaus, destroying the Seleucid camp while their army was off trying to find Judah's.

The Maccabean uprising lasted years, with both sides trading victories. Antiochus IV actually died during the rebellion (in 164 BCE), but during an unrelated military campaign against the Parthians. That same year, Judah's brother Eleazer fell during the Maccabean loss at the Battle of Beth-Zehariah, while he attacked a massive war elephant, crawling under the animal to kill it and dying when it collapsed on top of him. Eventually, the Maccabees proved enough of a consistent thorn in the Seleucids' side that the empire agreed to a compromise that restored religious freedom and allowed the Maccabees to rededicate the temple in Jerusalem. With Antiochus IV dead, his top commander withdrew, leaving Judea under nominal Seleucid rule but without any real enforcement.

Judah had won, but the victory didn't last long. Even once the Seleucids backed off, Judah and his men had to fight a series of battles against other Jews who

SPORTING SUCCESS

Judah Maccabee is so synonymous with the idea of Jewish strength that when Olympics-style games were created for Jewish athletes, organizers named them in honor of the revolutionary leader. Held every four years in Israel (formerly every three), the Maccabiah Games began as a response to European nations banning Jews from taking part in official sporting events. Since that time, they've become the largest international sports competition other than the Olympics and soccer's World Cup. Jewish athletes from more than eighty countries—and non-Jewish athletes who live in Israel—have participated in the Maccabiah Games.

The event has several ties to the area's revolutionary past. Though the idea originated a couple decades earlier, the games debuted in 1932, when the territory was again controlled by a major colonial power (in this case, Great Britain). The event was even timed to coincide with the 1,800th anniversary of yet another Jewish rebellion, the Bar Kokhba revolt against the Romans in 132–136 CE. Like the Olympics, the Maccabiah Games begin with a torch carried through the streets; this one always starts its journey in Modi'in, the birthplace of Judah Maccabee.

WHO ARE YOU?

American pop culture immortalized the gladiator in legendary director Stanley Kubrick's 1960 film *Spartacus*, starring Kirk Douglas in the title role and Sir Laurence Olivier as Crassus. Probably the most famous scene in the film depicts the Romans telling the captured slaves to turn over Spartacus, who stands up and bravely declares, "I am Spartacus!" One by one, the other slaves stand up and say the same, refusing to let Spartacus take the fall alone, and they all get crucified for their efforts.

It's a great scene, but not based on anything that actually happened (well, except the part where the Romans crucified lots of his men). The movie took that bit from the book it was based on, one written by Howard Fast. The author wrote his version of the Spartacus story while in prison for refusing to name names during Joseph McCarthy's witch hunt against supposed Communists in the entertainment industry, and the iconic scene is generally considered a tribute to those who refused to rat out their friends to save themselves.

Spartacus probably came from Thrace, a large area in eastern Greece, and at one time wound up fighting as part of a Roman auxiliary force. Whether he was a mercenary hired by the Romans or a captured fighter forced into service is unknown, but at some point Spartacus deserted, got captured, and was sold into slavery. The man who bought him ran a *ludus*, a school where gladiators were trained to fight, in Capua— and his military background made Spartacus an appealing gladiator.

In 73 BCE, some of the slaves in the *ludus* conspired to escape, and managed to convince a good number of the others. On one hand, the future gladiators were going to spend the rest of their lives fighting to the death against each other in an arena, just to entertain the citizens of the state that enslaved them. On the other, if they rebelled, their worst-case scenario would involve spending the rest of their lives fighting to the death against the Romans, and they could live free in the meantime. For enough of the slaves, it was an easy choice.

Somebody betrayed the plot, but seventy-eight of the gladiators still managed to escape, even though their only weapons were knives and other tools they found in the kitchen of the school. The escaped slaves then stole a transport of gladiator weapons and headed for the hills, setting up camp near Mount Vesuvius.

Spartacus was elected one of the new army's trio of leaders, along with two Gauls named Crixus and Oenomaus. Because he left no records behind and so little is known about him, it's hard to say exactly what Spartacus was rebelling against. He might have opposed slavery in general, or he might have

Spartacus fights on.

only cared about freeing slaves who were going to join his army. In any event, his forces regularly raided the countryside, stealing supplies and recruiting more troops.

This time, the Roman government didn't wait to react, but it did take the threat a tad too lightly. With its powerful legions out fighting other wars, Rome had a commander named Gaius Claudius Glaber recruit a militia to take care of the rebelling gladiators. It didn't work out well for Glaber. He tried to starve out Spartacus and his men, cutting off their escape route and trapping them on Vesuvius. The gladiators organized an attack in response, making ladders out of vines and paying a surprise visit to the Roman camp. Since they were trained gladiators, many of Spartacus's men were outstanding fighters, and they vanquished Glaber's less-experienced troops.

Defeating even a makeshift Roman force made Spartacus far more dangerous. Word of the rebellion spread, with thousands of slaves—and even some free Italian peasants—joining up. The troops also spent the winter of 73–72 BCE training to become a more organized army. Roman sources sometimes exaggerated the size of Rome's enemies (it looked better for the Romans), but Spartacus could have had between 70,000 and 100,000 people under his command.

In the spring of 72 BCE, the gladiators divided into two forces and left Vesuvius to fight their way out of Italy. Rome sent two legions after the split army, killing Crixus and defeating his share of the troops in southern Italy. Spartacus and his forces were on their way to the Alps when the two Roman armies approached his troops from different directions. Spartacus won this round, first attacking and defeating the army to his north, then turning around and beating the other one.

At this point, though, Spartacus made the mistake that ultimately led to his defeat. Nobody knows the reason why for certain, but he didn't cross the Alps when he reached them, and instead went back south into Italy. In hindsight, getting out of Italy seems like an obvious move. Instead, fighting Roman attacks along the way, he led his men down to the tip of Italy with a plan to cross the Strait of Messina and head for Sicily. He even made a deal with some Sicilian pirates to help his men cross but—either by betrayal or some complication—the pirates never showed up, leaving Spartacus and his men stuck in Italy.

———————

The slave army also had to face a new, more effective Roman adversary. Marcus Licinius Crassus, the richest man in Rome and one of its best generals, volunteered to lead an army to destroy Spartacus and his men. The two forces first faced off in a number of smaller battles, but by the spring of 71 BCE Crassus had Spartacus and his men pinned down in the toe of the boot of Italy, using a miles-long series of walls and ditches to lay siege to the former slaves. Surrounded, unable to get to Sicily, and aware that more Roman legions were on the way, Spartacus and his men took the offensive. One day in April, they unexpectedly attacked Crassus's army in the Battle of the Siler River. Whether they did so because they realized the odds against them were only going to get worse, or because they wished to die with honor, they charged the Romans on the battlefield and were predictably defeated in hand-to-hand combat.

Spartacus died in the battle, and his body was never found. In a way, he was lucky. Some of his troops escaped and fought a number of additional battles against the Romans, but all they did was delay the inevitable. About 6,000 of his men were captured alive by the Romans and crucified all along the Appian Way, the main road into Rome from Capua. Years after they died, their bodies were left up as reminders to visitors about what could happen to anyone who dared to rebel against Rome. ●

JULIUS CAESAR

THE TIME: *100–44 BCE*

THE PLACE: *Rome*

THE OPPONENT: *The Roman Senate*

I t can be difficult to think of Julius Caesar as one of the most important revolutionaries in history; after all, he spent quite a bit of his military career putting down revolutions against Roman rule. Still, his late-career decision to fight his own countrymen turned Rome from a quasi-democratic republic into an empire that would take its orders from just one man from that point forward.

Born in 100 BCE, Gaius Julius Caesar came from a respectable patrician family, but not one with historically strong political ties—until his aunt married Gaius Marius. When Caesar was still in his teens, Marius wound up fighting Rome's first and second civil wars against fellow former consul Lucius Cornelius Sulla (the first Roman commander to ever march against the city, and the first Roman to become dictator by force). Whoever had the upper hand for a time tried to purge the other's real or suspected supporters. Young Caesar was on Sulla's hit list, and had to flee the city under the dictator's rule. Caesar eventually received a pardon from Sulla, but even then he avoided Rome, instead joining the army and gaining experience that would come in handy later.

Caesar moved back to Rome once Sulla died, and soon became a popular figure among the *populares*, the Roman citizens of the middle and lower classes. At first, he made a name for himself as a lawyer and public speaker, but in his late twenties he began his political career. Caesar worked his way up the political ladder in Rome and publicly identified himself with the legacy of Marius, including supporting, as Marius did, expanding the benefits of citizenship to more Romans.

Fans of Caesars saw him as a genuine democratic reformer, while his opponents saw his populism as a naked power grab, a way of getting the common people of Rome to support him. Either way, winning one office after another,

VENI VIDI VICI

Caesar makes his appearance in Andrea Andreani's aptly named series "The Triumph of Julius Caesar."

Caesar successfully increased his profile, his support among the public, and his influence in the city.

———————

In 60 BCE, Caesar found a sly way to further increase his influence. He made a then-secret alliance with Crassus and Pompey—respectively, the richest man in Roman history, and Rome's best and most famous military leader. The two had been co-consuls in 70 BCE but had fallen out with each other before Caesar joined them in the political alliance later called the First Triumvirate. This way, they looked out for his interests and he looked out for theirs (even making the older Pompey his son-in-law through marriage). Combined, the three men were powerful enough to often work around the Senate's opposition to get what they wanted—the historian Livy later dubbed the Triumvirate "a conspiracy against the state by its three leading citizens."

In 59 BCE, with the help of Pompey and Crassus, Caesar won election as one of the two consuls Rome chose every year. In that role, Caesar made plenty of enemies, as he and his colleagues went around the law by often ignoring the Senate (and Caesar's ineffective co-consul) or blatantly influencing specific senators to do what they wanted. When his term neared its end, Caesar knew his political rivals were licking their chops to bring charges against him. Roman leaders remained safe from prosecution while in certain offices, so he used his alliances to get an appointment as a governor in Gaul. This way, he could not only stay in a safe office, but he could also erase the large debt he'd acquired as consul, all the while keeping his influence back home through the Triumvirate.

In the first decade after his official consulship, Caesar and his legions conquered enemies over and over again, greatly increasing both Roman territory and Caesar's personal fortune. That stretch saw him conquer Gaul, fight off some German tribes, and even invade Britain. Perhaps better than any man of his era, Caesar understood the importance of public opinion and of controlling his public image. While on campaign in Gaul, he published annual books detailing his adventures. Many of those exploits were considered war crimes under Roman law, but Caesar had the standing back home to get away with it.

However, the same period saw the end of the Triumvirate—and with it, his immunity to the rules. In 53 BCE, Crassus died while on a military campaign against the Parthians, and Caesar's strongest tie to Pompey disappeared when

CROSSING OVER

Caesar's move to cross the Rubicon qualified as bold enough to cross into our language. "Crossing the Rubicon" is now generally used to signify a bold action that, once undertaken, cannot be abandoned or reversed.

HAIL CAESAR

Julius Caesar's name continued long after death, and what began as just his family surname became a title for those who followed. The first few emperors to use "Caesar" as part of their name had actually inherited it, because Caesar adopted Octavian in his will and the name passed along that way. However, Rome's fourth emperor, Claudius, assigned it to himself as a title when he took power, and it became precedent that the name "Caesar" now meant any emperor of Rome.

With how far the Roman Empire spread, the use of the name spread throughout Europe. The longtime title of German leaders ("Kaiser") and of Russian leaders ("Czar") both originated as translations of "Caesar" and remained in use, respectively, until the end of World War I and the Bolshevik Revolution during the same war.

his daughter Julia died. Meanwhile, the Senate had grown more and more terrified of Caesar's power. So, when his term as governor ended in 50 BCE, the Senate ordered Caesar to disband his legions and return to Rome. He knew that probably meant prosecution, so he refused.

In January 49 BCE, Caesar made his riskiest and boldest move by crossing the Rubicon, the river that served as the boundary between Rome and its frontier. Under Roman law, generals were not allowed to bring their armies into the city (unless authorized to do so for a specific reason). Caesar knew crossing the Rubicon would mean war and—allegedly after saying, "The die is cast"—he brought his legion into Italy and drove Rome into crisis. The Senate immediately declared war on Caesar and ordered his former ally Pompey to defend the republic's interests.

Any doubts anyone had about Caesar as a military leader were soon erased. After all, now he wasn't beating tribal armies; he was beating Roman legionaries led by one of history's greatest generals. He also made a point of showing mercy to Romans (and only Romans) captured in battle, allowing them to join his forces.

Caesar defeated Pompey decisively in 48 BCE at the Battle of Pharsalus in Central Greece, despite being vastly outnumbered and lacking his adversary's fortified position. Pompey fled to Egypt, where he was murdered by the pharaoh's men, and—after placing some allies in power in Rome—Caesar followed him there, where he began his political and personal relationship with Cleopatra (see page 34). He fought smaller battles against Pompey loyalists in Spain, and soon had no meaningful opposition.

Caesar's victory clinched a new order for Rome, and he made sure people knew it. He named himself dictator and began to rewrite the Roman constitution. He appointed his supporters to the Senate, turning what used to be the real power in Roman government into a rubber stamp for his proposals. He broke with tradition by giving the dictatorship a number of new judicial powers. Some of his moves—such as erasing many large debts and building public works—were popular with the masses. Still, his perceived arrogance made him many enemies in the Senate and elsewhere.

He had already extended his term as dictator several times, but naming himself dictator for life in February of 44 BCE seemed the final straw for a number of senators, who began to plot his overthrow. Caesar was murdered on March 15 of 44 BCE (the "Ides of March"), the day a seer had warned him would bring danger. Just as he was about to enter a Senate meeting, he was suddenly surrounded by about sixty senators and stabbed to death.

If Caesar's power grab didn't technically end the Roman Republic, the aftermath of his death certainly did. At his funeral, mobs of lower-class Romans, many of whom saw Caesar as their champion, held massive demonstrations and even tried attacking the homes of his killers. The power vacuum after his death caused a series of civil wars. Octavian, Caesar's named heir, teamed up with Marc Antony to fight a war against Brutus and Cassius, ringleaders of the assassination. They then turned on each other, with Octavian defeating Antony and Cleopatra, Caesar's former lover. Within seventeen years of Julius Caesar's death, Octavian had consolidated power, renamed himself Caesar Augustus, declared himself emperor for life, and permanently replaced the Roman Republic with a Roman Empire. ●

VERCINGETORIX

THE TIME: *c. 82–46 BCE*

THE PLACE: *Gaul*

THE OPPONENT: *Rome*

By the time Julius Caesar made it his mission to conquer the Gauls for good, Romans had been conquering the tribal peoples of the area for centuries. In 52 BCE, one chieftain organized a valiant last stand, uniting the Gauls under his banner. It didn't work, but it did make Vercingetorix a national hero in France.

The area known as Gaul in the ancient world included what's now France, plus Belgium, Luxembourg, and parts of Germany, Italy, Switzerland, and the Netherlands. As for the Gauls, they began as Celtic peoples who spread

Vercingetorix and his very sensitive horse surrender to Caesar in this 1899 painting by Lionel Royer.

throughout the territory and mixed with other tribes. While they would sometimes team up in wars, however, the Gauls never had a central leader or government, and instead functioned as a bunch of separate tribes with their own territories and cultures.

To Rome, that diversity was a weakness it could exploit.

Rome's first major war against Gallic peoples started about 390 BCE, when the Senones tribe invaded Roman territory and marched on the city before Rome prevailed in a tough battle. Tensions between Gauls and Romans never really improved, and the next two centuries saw more than half a dozen major wars in Italy between the factions. Gallic tribes also joined others to fight against Romans; Hannibal, for example, used mercenaries from Gaul and recruited Gauls in Italy to his side during the Second Punic War. Suffice it to say, none of this made the Gauls terribly popular in Rome. By around 225 BCE, the fed-up Roman Senate made it a goal to drive the Gauls out of Italy, leaving the Alps as a natural dividing line—a plan that, for the most part, succeeded.

A new round of Roman-Gallic wars west of the Alps kicked off in 58 BCE, started by none other than Julius Caesar (see page 25), fresh off serving as consul and now governor of multiple Gallic lands Rome controlled. In his own journals from the time, Caesar portrayed his conquest of the surrounding area as a preemptive strike against an enemy who had caused trouble in the past. Less-charitable historians see it as an attempt by Caesar to make some money to pay the debts he racked up as consul, and to pad his résumé with another big military win.

Some Gallic tribes were willing to negotiate treaties with Rome, and some even asked for Roman help against mutual enemies (mostly German tribes to the east). Others tried to stand up to Rome, but Caesar and his legions crushed them. In the winter of 54–53 BCE, Caesar wiped out most of the Eburones in retaliation for that tribe attacking a Roman garrison.

Vercingetorix, a chieftain of the Arverni tribe, saw Rome picking off Gallic opposition and knew Caesar would soon force his people into either defeat or surrender. Though the Gauls had a long history of refusing to function as a unified people—Vercingetorix's own father, Celtillus, was executed for attempting to expand his leadership to more of Gaul—he believed a multi-tribe Gallic army represented the only shot at survival.

In 52 BCE, at an annual gathering of the tribes, Vercingetorix made his case for rebelling against Rome before it grew too late. Even Caesar, in his own writings, admitted the Gauls were "smarting" from their powerlessness against Rome, and Vercingetorix convinced many that an armed uprising was the only way to take power back. His supporters declared him king of the Arverni, and several

CLEOPATRA

THE TIME: *69–30 BCE*

THE PLACE: *Egypt*

THE OPPONENTS: *Her brother, then Rome*

In modern times, Cleopatra is often remembered mostly for her legendary beauty or her tragic demise. In her day, however, she earned her fame as a major political player on the world stage. Cleopatra was a savvy military strategist and diplomat, overthrowing her brother to become the only sole female ruler of her time, and the last pharaoh of the Nile kingdom.

Though born a princess in Egypt, Cleopatra was a Greek woman, a direct descendant of one of Alexander the Great's top generals. When Alexander's commanders carved up his empire after his death, Ptolemy took over Egypt and established a dynasty there, declaring it the Ptolemaic Kingdom in 305 BCE and naming himself pharaoh. To ensure the legitimacy of the bloodline, the Ptolemaic pharaohs (all of them named Ptolemy) married their sisters, so for generations Egyptian rulers came from an incestuous family of Macedonian Greeks.

Unlike some of the other Alexander-based dynasties, the Ptolemys didn't impose Greek culture on their territories, and instead let Egyptians be Egyptian and worship their own gods (though the Ptolemys never adopted much of their subjects' culture). After the first three Ptolemys, however, the dynasty lost a lot of its prestige and power, with a mix of scandals, corruption, and a string of succession-driven murders leaving Egypt weak at home and internationally.

Cleopatra's father, Ptolemy XII, had ruled during a particularly turbulent period marked by uprisings among the Egyptians, territories given up, and Egypt's need to ally with Rome to avoid attacks from other kingdoms. When he died in 51 BCE, Cleopatra became the queen of Egypt at only eighteen. The Ptolemys' family-relations policy made her younger brother, Ptolemy XIII, pharaoh. Though he was only ten years old, tradition made him not only Cleopatra's co-ruler, but also her husband.

Cleopatra, marbleized.

For a little while, Cleopatra managed to rule Egypt without much interference from her brother/husband, handling all official business herself and even coining money with the image of her face rather than his. Cleopatra made a point of becoming the first of her family line to make an effort to learn the Egyptian language, and applied the same savvy approach by taking part in Egyptian religious rituals. Pharaohs had always claimed to be gods themselves, and Cleopatra specifically associated herself with the Egyptian goddess Isis, one of the most fervently worshipped at the time (she possibly even claimed to be Isis's reincarnation). By the standards of the aloof Ptolemys, she was almost a woman of the people.

This made her a more legitimate queen in the eyes of many Egyptians—and a threat to powerful interests in Alexandria, the capital city. Her brother's advisors, led by a eunuch named Pothinus, decided that Cleopatra had to go. In 48 BCE, they drove her from the capital and made Ptolemy XIII the sole ruler, with a lot of influence from these same advisors.

Cleopatra refused to take her exile in stride, and organized a rebellion to reclaim her power. She set up a base in Pelusium on the Sinai Peninsula and started recruiting her own army, using her money and influence to put together a force of Egyptians and foreign mercenaries. However, she lacked the resources of the capital. Ptolemy and his cronies did whatever they could to deny her supplies, even banning shipments of grain to any part of the kingdom except Alexandria itself. She managed to camp her army near the city, but she knew she had no real chance of taking it.

Cleopatra's big break came when Julius Caesar (see page 25), still fighting his own civil war, arrived in Alexandria in 48 BCE. Shortly before Caesar's arrival, men loyal to Ptolemy and Pothinus had betrayed Caesar's rival Pompey, killing the great Roman general when he came to get help. Ptolemy expected Caesar to reward him, but the murder of a man he respected only angered Caesar. Cleopatra saw an opportunity, but her brother—still hoping to persuade Caesar to take his side—had the Roman's residence guarded so that she couldn't get to him.

Cleopatra had to sneak into Alexandria in order to meet Caesar and convince him to join her cause. The story goes that the young queen made a particularly memorable entrance by having herself rolled up in a large rug and delivered to Caesar's quarters, then unrolled in private. Soon, she and Caesar were a team, in both politics and romance. Ptolemy took the arrangement predictably badly, and put Caesar and his small detachment of troops under siege in Alexandria for nearly six months. Caesar's allies sent reinforcements, and the whole thing exploded into civil war.

At the Battle of the Nile in 47 BCE, Cleopatra and Caesar personally led their combined armies against Ptolemy XIII, who drowned in the Nile while fleeing the battle. Victorious, Cleopatra regained the throne (alongside her even-younger brother, Ptolemy XIV, who was too young to wield any power, and whom she married purely as a nod to tradition).

She and Caesar never married, as Roman law wouldn't recognize a union with a non-Roman, but their affair continued for more than a decade and Cleopatra moved to Rome with him. She also gave birth to Caesar's only known biological son, Caesarion (technically named Ptolemy Caesar). After Caesar's murder in 44 BCE, Cleopatra returned to Egypt. Her brother/co-ruler died mysteriously (possibly after being poisoned by by Cleopatra), and she made Caesarion her new co-ruler.

Even while in Egypt, Cleopatra remained involved in Rome's internal politics, which ultimately cost her. In 41 BCE, she began an affair with Marc Antony, one of the leaders of post-Caesar Rome. Antony clearly fell for Cleopatra, as the pair had three children together and Antony left his wife to relocate to Egypt and marry his lover. In the process, he also used Roman armies to help Cleopatra expand Egypt's territory, and publicly decreed Caesarion to be Caesar's rightful heir.

This ticked off Octavian, the man Caesar had named his heir in his will and Antony's biggest political rival in Rome. Octavian and his supporters began an anti-Cleopatra propaganda campaign,

A DESIRABLE ROLE

Cleopatra's status as the most famous woman of her day—and her legendary romances with some of the era's most powerful men—has made her a subject of theater and film for centuries. William Shakespeare's *Antony and Cleopatra*, one of his most popular and most acclaimed tragedies, debuted about 1606 and kept the story of Cleopatra in the public consciousness.

Within just a few years of the invention of motion pictures, Cleopatra became a popular subject for movies, starting with a 1908 filmed version of the Shakespeare play. Since then, actresses including Vivien Leigh, Claudette Colbert, and Elizabeth Taylor have taken turns playing the last queen of Egypt.

A BITING THEORY

As an important part of her legend, Cleopatra's suicide by the bite of an asp carried some valuable subtext. The asp, a snake now called the Egyptian cobra, had sacred meaning as a symbol of the goddess Isis. And Cleopatra made her last act a suicide fit for a queen, reclining on a golden couch while wearing fine clothing and jewelry. Octavian tried to deny her the death she chose, even having snake charmers suck the poison from her wound.

The story of the asp bite was questioned even in ancient times, as no snake was found in her chambers. Ancient historians suggested the poison could have come from a comb, from an ointment, or even from Cleopatra biting her own skin and putting snake poison in the wound. There's no sure answer, but most Roman sources go with the snakebite explanation, and Octavian gave it an official endorsement when he held a Triumph parade in Rome that depicted Cleopatra with an asp biting her.

portraying the Egyptian queen as a seductress and a potential threat to Rome, and claiming that she used Antony to grow her power. Her affair with Caesar had already caused a scandal in Rome, so it was relatively easy for Octavian to turn the public against the influence of a foreign queen.

In 33 BCE, Octavian got the Senate to declare war on Egypt, thereby setting out to conquer it. The decisive Battle of Actium took place on September 2, 31 BCE, when a combined naval force led by Antony and Cleopatra was overwhelmingly defeated off the coast of Greece. Cleopatra retreated back to Egypt and began frantically preparing for the coming invasion, sending Caesarion away for his own safety. Antony, wrongly believing Cleopatra had died in the battle, stabbed himself in a suicide attempt, and died soon after his men brought him back to Egypt.

On August 1, 30 BCE, Octavian captured Alexandria. Rather than suffer whatever fate he had planned for her, Cleopatra committed suicide on August 12, supposedly by the bite of a poisonous asp. She was only thirty-nine years old.

To remove any chance of Cleopatra's line continuing, Octavian (either through bribery or trickery) managed to have Caesarion brought back to Egypt and executed. Octavian declared Egypt a province of Rome that same year, and installed Roman governors. The death of Cleopatra also meant the death of the Ptolemaic Dynasty that had ruled Egypt for three centuries, and the birth of Roman rule in one of the ancient world's most sought-after territories. •

ARMINIUS

THE TIME: *c. 18 BCE–19 CE*

THE PLACE: *Germania*

THE OPPONENT: *Rome*

Some of the toughest military leaders in history (more than a few of them in this book) took on Rome and suffered for it. For a good stretch of history, the spread of the Roman Empire really looked unstoppable, as the constantly expanding power seemed destined to take over all of Europe and the Mediterranean. That he stood up to the Romans during that era and walked away victorious made Arminius revolutionary among revolutionaries.

Arminius knew a lot about how the Romans operated, because he basically grew up as one of them. In the ancient world, it was common practice for the winning side in a war to demand high-born children from the defeated state as hostages. The children were usually raised well, often as friends of their captors' children, but there was always the threat of harm if their parents' homeland didn't obey the victorious nation. Born about 18 BCE, Arminius was the son of the Cheruscan leader Segimerus and became a hostage at a young age, a warning to his father not to try anything funny.

By that time, Rome had been fighting German tribes for quite a while. A pair of Germanic peoples, the Cimbri and the Teutones, had given the Romans a scare less than a century before Arminius's birth. In just a few years, the Cimbri had gone from a people nobody in Rome had ever heard of to an invading force that killed more than 100,000 Roman troops before they were defeated in 101 BCE. As they had with other tribal peoples like the Celts and the Gauls, the Romans took on individual tribes whenever possible, conquering some in battle and turning others into relatively powerless client states.

While growing up a hostage in Rome, Arminius benefitted from a formal Roman military education. In fact, he was so assimilated that he gained Roman citizenship that, combined with his noble birth, let him achieve status as an "equestrian," the Roman equivalent of a knight. Arminius excelled at his military training, and the Romans put him in charge of some auxiliary forces, collections of non-Roman troops that fought along with the legions.

At some point, Arminius decided to turn on his hosts and lead his own people against them. It's unclear whether this was a sudden decision or if he'd essentially been a double agent for a while, learning the Roman ways specifically to use their strengths against them. Either way, he grew tired of watching Europe's most powerful empire dominating Germania and hatched a plan to do something about it.

He was somewhere around twenty-seven years old when he set in motion one of the ancient world's legendary victories in September of 9 CE. Depending on whose side is telling the story, Arminius either executed a brilliant strategy or pulled off a dirty trick, convincing Rome's governor in Germany, Publius Quinctilius Varus, to lead his three legions into the Teutoburg Forest—and into a carefully laid trap.

Varus was known as a notoriously vicious governor, a reputation he brought with him from stints as governor of Roman Africa and, later, Syria. He knew there were reports of rebellion in northern Germania; after all, Arminius had recently led a Roman auxiliary force into the region, ostensibly to keep the rebels under control.

NAMING RIGHTS

Centuries after his death, Arminius got a new name, one that Germans have continued to use for another few centuries. Supposedly, the idea of rechristening him from Arminius to Hermann came from none other than Martin Luther (see page 59), because he thought that the original version was just a Latin form of a German moniker. Whether he was right is still up in the air.

In the 1800s, when the state of Prussia began the process of forming a modern state of Germany, Arminius/Hermann became a powerful symbol. After victory in the Franco-Prussian War, the Germans completed the Hermannsdenkmal memorial in 1875. Located in the Teutoburg Forest, the statue showing Arminius with a raised sword is still one of Germany's most well-known tourist attractions.

One of the tallest copper statues in the United States is New York City's Hermann Heights Monument, built by The Order of the Sons of Hermann, a group started in the 1800s to help German immigrants. The town of Hermann, Missouri, was also founded specifically as a place for German expats to settle. Rightly or wrongly, the Hermann name has been used a lot.

What Varus didn't realize was that Arminius was actually one of the rebels, and that he had gone back to northern Germania to gain allies for his stand against Rome. Along with his own auxiliary troops—Rome had put him in charge of Germanic soldiers, including members of his own tribe—Arminius made an appeal to other tribes in the region to send him men. Only a few agreed, but that still provided the numbers needed.

Once ready, Arminius returned to Varus, convinced the gullible governor that his legions were needed to fight the rebellion, and went with them to the scene of the alleged unrest. Varus had three full legions, totaling about 20,000 men with him, and few would leave the Teutoburg Forest alive.

Arminius had his troops hidden in the forest along both sides of a narrow trail, and led the Romans directly into the ambush. His forces began by surrounding the legions, attacking with light swords and javelins. The Romans tried to break out, only to wind up in another trap Arminius had prepared, with the escape route cut off by a trench and a huge wall the Germans could hide behind. Fleeing Romans were chased down by Arminius's cavalry, while the rest of his men attacked the tired Romans in the field. In just four days of intense fighting, the Germans won a decisive victory. Varus fell on his sword, literally, choosing suicide over the embarrassment of returning to Rome after such a crushing defeat.

This is definitely a Roman bust. However, it may or may not be a Roman bust of Arminius. (Experts disagree.)

The Roman historian Tacitus called Arminius "without doubt Germania's liberator," and he is often credited with forcing Rome to give up on conquering Germania. That overstates things a bit. Arminius didn't unite the German tribes, and just a few tribes contributed men to his uprising. Rome also didn't give up on taking Germania. The battle stopped them from truly conquering east of the Rhine River, but Roman forces were again fighting battles in the area within a few years of the Teutoburg disaster, and they didn't withdraw completely from Germania for much longer. Still, Arminius won a huge and important upset.

CAPTURED IN SONG

Few cultures composed better classical music and opera than the Germans, and with Arminius's status as an epic German hero, it makes sense that composers wrote epic operas about him.

In the 1690s, Heinrich Ignaz Franz von Biber composed *Arminio*, a highly fictionalized account that became the first opera performed in the opera hotspot of Salzburg. This version has the Roman leader Germanicus enslaving Arminius's wife and selling her to Tiberius, and Arminius disguising himself as a servant in order to rescue her. The opera's subtitle, *Chia la Dura la Vince*, translates as "He Who Endures, Triumphs," an apt slogan for Arminius and his story. Then George Frideric Handel (best known for his *Messiah*) created his own *Arminio* in 1736. His work featured the famous castrated soprano Conti playing the role of Arminius, who spends a good chunk of the opera in chains, even though the real Arminius was a hostage, not a slave, and was never captured by Rome after his victory in the Teutoburg Forest.

Neither version is all that accurate, but they do make for good stories.

Unfortunately for Arminius, life got rougher after Teutoburg. The Romans retaliated by capturing his pregnant wife, making her and her unborn son slaves for life. Another Roman commander, Germanicus, led several effective attacks against Arminius and his forces. The Romans never got him, but other members of his tribe feared his power, and murdered Arminius in 19 CE.

His legacy, it's fair to say, survived him. Rome never managed to fully conquer Germany, and—though internal problems probably made it inevitable—it was Germanic "barbarians" who dealt the final blow when the Roman Empire fell. ●

BOUDICA

THE TIME: *c. 30–61*

THE PLACE: *Britain*

THE OPPONENT: *Rome*

Revolution in the ancient world was mostly a man's game, probably because few ancient societies allowed women to serve as leaders. This makes Boudica that much more impressive, as the queen of the Iceni tribe survived a brutal betrayal and rallied the Britons to fight the invaders of their homeland.

Despite living in the first century CE as a Celtic woman under Roman rule in the south of what's now Great Britain, Boudica actually had every expectation of being able to live peacefully with Rome. During this conquest of the British Isles, Rome had taken its normal divide-and-conquer approach, making agreements with friendly tribes, and the Iceni were on that list.

The invasion of Britain had started in 55 BCE with Julius Caesar, who set up client states but never established a true military occupation. Later emperors changed that, though several planned invasions were canceled when the Romans had to turn their attention to uprisings in other parts of the empire. In 43 CE, the emperor Claudius began a real power grab in Britain, sending legions to invade. It supposedly took only sixteen days for the emperor to claim victory over the southern part of the island and install a governor. Prasutagus, Boudica's husband and the king of the Iceni, chose to make a deal with the Romans. They would let him continue his rule as long as he cooperated with their way of doing things.

Other Celtic peoples, particularly in Wales, took less kindly to Roman rule and started to rebel, though not terribly successfully. The Iceni instead kept to their deal, even after Claudius died and his chosen replacement—his famously sadistic great-nephew Nero—took over the job of emperor. Nero gave his governor in

ROYAL REVIVALS

With Boudica's status as a woman warrior who united the British, it made sense that her legend twice got significant boosts from woman warriors uniting the British in their own rights.

Boudica's story got a revival under Queen Elizabeth I, when the Tudor queen successfully defended her kingdom against the mighty Spanish armada. James Aske's 1588 poem "Elizabetha Triumphans" compared Elizabeth to Boudica, while numerous histories of England written around that time tell Boudica's story. Petruccio Ubaldini's "The Lives of the Noble Ladies of the Kingdom of England and Scotland," published in 1591, presented the Iceni queen as a righteous fighter against tyranny, while John Fletcher's 1610 play *Bonduca* also drew parallels between its subject and the recently deceased Elizabeth.

Another revival came during the reign of Queen Victoria, who was a big fan of Boudica and saw some of herself in her. (For example, she pointed out that both of their names were versions of the word "victory.") Around this time, stories popped up, such as that of Boudica being buried beneath King's Cross Station in London (almost certainly false); historians began updating her name to Boudicea; and a statue of her was commissioned in 1905 and built right near Parliament.

Queen Victoria's fascination with her Celtic predecessor was a bit ironic, as Victoria ruled during the peak of British world domination—a time often described as the sun never setting on the British Empire—when the queen's situation more closely mirrored that of the Romans than that of the rebel Britons.

Britain more leeway, and Roman rule became far more difficult to endure. Complaints among the Iceni included Roman troops stealing from them, kidnapping children to turn into soldiers, and forcing Celts to join the army. Still, the deal between the Iceni king and the emperor held things together, at least in theory.

That changed in 60 CE, when Prasutagus died. His final wish was to split his kingdom in half, with half going to his two daughters and the other half to Nero. Even though this gave him half a kingdom without his having to do anything, the emperor wasn't satisfied.

The Romans were an even more male-dominated society than the Celts, and they only recognized inheritance and succession through the male line. Nero didn't care for Prasutagus's divided will, and viewed the idea of any land going to the daughters as illegitimate. In his typically cruel way, he took his anger out on Boudica and her family. Both daughters were raped by Roman troops, while the queen was publicly stripped naked and flogged. Other Iceni had to pay too,

LONDON'S BURNING

Much of what historians know about Boudica comes from Roman sources or from stories passed down by her fans. Her famous burning of Londinium, however, has also been confirmed by scientists and archaeologists.

Even today, nearly 2,000 years after Boudica's rebellion, builders in London find evidence of her attack on the city in a layer of reddish ash, dated to that time period and presumably made up of the people and buildings that burned in 61, which still sits below London. Much of the city burned again in 1666, in a blaze that started more innocently, in a bakery, and killed far fewer people despite massive property damage. That makes today's London the third version of a major city built on that spot. The same kind of ashen evidence also backs up her destruction of Camulodunum (which is now Colchester) and Verulamium (now St. Albans).

as Nero claimed Prasutagus owed Rome money and chose to hold the dead ruler's people responsible for the alleged debt. He took the lands of other Iceni nobles and began to rule them the same way he ruled those of tribes that had never made a deal.

In the words of the Roman historian Tacitus, the Britons were "broken in to obedience, not to slavery." This mistreatment of their queen qualified as the kind of insult that couldn't stand, and Celts used to having a degree of self-rule had no intention of giving that up so easily. Boudica was obviously enraged, and the other Iceni understood Rome was asserting itself as a permanent conqueror. The Iceni joined forces with another tribe, the Trinovantes, and made Boudica their war leader.

The Iceni queen opened her rebellion with a bold move. While Rome's governor was off fighting in Wales, she marched on Camulodunum, the Roman provincial capital. The Romans had pushed many native people from that city and taken over their homes, and forced the local Celts to pay for the building of the Temple of Claudius, a particularly offensive move. Boudica attacked the city, burning some buildings and destroying others. Fittingly, her army drove the last of the defense forces into the notorious temple before she destroyed it and killed those inside.

In case destroying the local capital wasn't enough to make Rome take her seriously, Boudica moved on to Londinium, the site of modern London. The city was a growing trade stop, but the Roman governor—knowing he was outnumbered and that Boudica was a real threat—evacuated those he could and left the city to be destroyed. Boudica and her forces swept in, killing everyone they found and burning the city to the ground. For good measure, she did the same to the city of Verulamium.

By then, Boudica's army had put enough of a scare into the Romans that the infamous Nero strongly considered withdrawing from Britain entirely. As Tacitus put it, "Neither before nor since has Britain ever been in a more uneasy or dangerous state." Boudica killed between 70,000 and 80,000 Romans and allies, including a few thousand elite Roman soldiers.

Boudica, mid-harangue, in a 1793 painting by John Opie.

Like many of the revolutionaries who took on Rome, however, Boudica was well equipped to win battles but unable to win the war. While she was destroying Verulamium, the Roman governor Gaius Suetonius Paulinus was preparing what troops he had left to fight the much-larger Celtic army. He chose a battle site somewhere along Watling Street, the road between Verulamium and Londinium, and waited for the enemy to arrive.

Boudica and her daughters led the rebels into battle on a chariot, but the Romans fought off the first attack by throwing heavy javelins. Holding formation, Suetonius's forces were able to draw the Iceni and their allies into close quarters and then charge them with infantry, killing even the women and children traveling with the army. The Britons tried to retreat at one point, but they couldn't get past their own wagons and animals, allowing the Romans to attack from behind.

Boudica did not survive the battle, though exactly how she died remains a mystery. Depending on which source is right, she might have died from an illness, or she might have committed suicide as a way to avoid capture. Either way, she was gone by the time the Romans claimed victory and proceeded to march north. Her rebellion had lasted only about a year, but it forced Rome to reconsider its treatment of Britain in order to avoid creating another Boudica. Rome replaced its governors there with less-oppressive officials, and ruled with a lighter hand for most of the next few hundred years. ●

WILLIAM WALLACE

THE TIME: *c. 1270–1305*

THE PLACE: *Scotland*

THE OPPONENT: *England*

The Scottish struggle for independence against English rule didn't end with William Wallace, but his success in the early days of the war made him a legend in his lifetime and a folk hero in Scotland more than 700 years later.

England and Scotland had a period of relative peace with one another when Wallace was born, but in 1290, the heir to the Scottish throne died with no successor. Multiple candidates laid claim to it, giving the eventual king, John de Balliol, a weak position—many of his powers were ceded to a governing council of Scottish nobles. King Edward I shattered the peace between the two states in 1296, taking advantage of that weakness and invading.

English forces quickly sacked the Scottish city of Berwick and defeated a Scottish army at the Battle of Dunbar, and those actions forced King John to abdicate and cede the throne. Edward threw the deposed king in jail in the notorious Tower of London, held other Scottish nobles as prisoners of war, and immediately declared himself the king of Scotland. He demanded that the Scottish nobles still in power declare allegiance to him, giving England control over most of Scotland in just a few months. He also taxed the Scots heavily, forced Scottish men to fight in his army, and generally treated Scotland more like a feudal state than the free land it had been.

Not much is known about Wallace's life before Edward's invasion of Scotland other than a few basic facts. He was the son of a minor Scottish noble and land-owner. He was born in the 1270s, making him in his mid- to late twenties when

BRAVEHEART

Wallace's story got the big-screen treatment in 1995, with director/star Mel Gibson's *Braveheart*, which won multiple Oscars, including Best Picture. Like nearly any popular entertainment based on true events, the film took significant liberties with the story. Among the differences? It set Wallace's childhood during English occupation, when England didn't invade until just before the rebellion. It showed Wallace and the Scots wearing kilts, which they didn't wear for a few more centuries.

Much of the movie was based on an epic poem *The Wallace*, written in the 1400s by a bard known only as Blind Harry (or Henry the Minstrel). Though it was probably performed first, the poem was printed in 1488, and for a long time it sold more copies in Scotland than any book except the Bible.

he began his rebellion. And he probably had at least some military experience.

His emergence as an important figure came in May 1297, when he led about thirty men against Lanark Castle and killed the English sheriff in charge of Lanark in the first step of the Scottish War for Independence. Some stories say the sheriff had planned to arrest Wallace for one of several crimes (depending on the story), and that he arrested and executed Wallace's wife—which might not be true, but certainly would have given Wallace a motive.

Whatever the reason, the killing of the sheriff placed Wallace in open rebellion against the crown. Thousands of Scots joined him, while others carried out their own rebellion in the north. Wallace based his forces in Ettrick Forest in the south, from which he carried out guerilla-style raids against English towns. Edward had been occupied with his war in France (fought in part by forcibly drafted Scots), but he suddenly found himself having to deal with a Scotland-wide uprising.

Wallace won an important battle on September 11, 1297, despite being badly outnumbered. He and his army were stationed across the Forth River from the English garrison, so the English had to cross the river in order to attack. Wallace turned away negotiators and prepared for the English to cross the narrow bridge across the Forth, watching from a hillside. Once enough knights and heavy cavalry crossed, he and his men charged with spears, driving the heavier English forces back as other troops were crossing, and the bridge collapsed under the combined weight.

The Battle of Stirling Bridge saw the Scots kill about 5,000 English soldiers, including their hated treasurer (whose skin, after he was flayed alive, was reportedly turned into a belt for Wallace's sword). The Scots quickly took Stirling Castle, killing or driving off its English defenders.

William Wallace with his eyes on Hollywood. (They could take his life, but they could never take... his beard off!)

Wallace's efforts earned him a knighthood from the council of nobles who ruled Scotland, and they named him Guardian of Scotland in the name of the deposed King John. As the acting leader of the state, he sent word to European nations declaring Scotland's independence, and then took his military on the offensive to invade the north of England and lay siege to some northern towns.

On the one hand, Wallace's military success managed to unite most of Scotland's people. On the other, it also united the leadership of England, turning nobles who had been plotting against Edward into loyal supporters in fear of a common enemy. Edward returned from France to personally lead an army north, and put together a force of more than 13,000 men. The army included archers armed with a revolutionary new weapon that would soon become a staple of English warfare—the longbow.

Part of Wallace's strategy was to force English troops to head deeper into Scottish territory. So, before heading back to Scotland from his victories, he carried out a scorched-earth plan that gave Edward little in the way of supplies. Wallace succeeded in drawing the English forces onto his own turf, but Edward arrived at the Scottish camp near Falkirk in July 1298 with an army and strategy Wallace couldn't match.

Wallace's men held off the first charge of English knights, using their tight battle formations and long spears. Edward's archers won the day, however, with their longbows able to fire into Scottish formations from a safe distance and their arrows able to pierce Scottish armor and shields. In the chaos this caused, some Scottish nobles fled the battle and Wallace's formations broke. He and some survivors managed to escape into a nearby forest, but most of his army was destroyed in a crushing defeat.

The loss at Falkirk got Wallace a demotion from his leadership role—some stories say he resigned, others that he was replaced—and he instead went abroad as an envoy in search of aid for the Scottish cause. While he was away, key Scottish nobles—including John Comyn and Robert the Bruce, who, combined, had replaced Wallace as Guardian of Scotland—made deals with the English crown and recognized Edward as king in exchange for peace. By 1304, Edward was back in control of Scotland, and he offered a huge reward for Wallace's capture.

On August 5, 1305, Wallace was arrested near Glasgow by English soldiers and brought to London for what was basically a show trial—he wasn't allowed to speak or present evidence—on charges of treason and war crimes. With the guilty verdict decided from the start, Wallace still vocally denied the treason charge, saying he couldn't betray an English king to whom he had never had any allegiance. On August 23, he was stripped naked and dragged by horses to Smithfield. There, he was executed via an elaborate series of drawn-out tortures that included hanging him to the brink of death, then removing body parts while he was still alive, and ultimately beheading and quartering him.

If killing Wallace was designed to end Scottish opposition, the plan backfired by turning him into a martyr for a cause others would take up. After a brief peace, Robert the Bruce led the Scots in another war against English rule in 1328. His uprising ended with the Treaty of Edinburgh-Northampton, which gave Scotland the independence for which Wallace had given his life, though even that peace lasted only a few years before the Scots waged yet another war for independence. ●

UNION LABEL

Scottish independence lasted on and off for a few centuries after Wallace's death, but intermarriage between English and Scottish monarchs left the two states under one king in 1603. Several attempts were made to join the two lands more officially, which ultimately happened with the passage of the Acts of Union in 1707, which combined the English and Scottish parliaments into a new parliament of Great Britain. The iconic Union Jack design of the UK flag reflects that union, combining the red St. George's cross of the English flag on top of the white-on-blue St. Andrew's cross of Scotland's (and the cross of St. Patrick for Ireland, but that's a whole other matter).

OWAIN GLYNDWR

THE TIME: *c. 1354–c. 1415*

THE PLACE: *Wales*

THE OPPONENT: *England*

Owain Glyndwr often gets compared to folk legends of early Britain—characters like Robin Hood or King Arthur. To this day, he remains a national hero in his native Wales, since he was the man who led the last real shot at keeping his homeland independent and was the last native Welshman to serve as its prince.

By the time Glyndwr was born, in the 1350s, the island of Britain had endured plenty of invasions and conquests. Originally settled by Celtic peoples long before there was written history, the island had already experienced Roman rule, invasions by several Germanic tribes, and attacks by Vikings from Scandinavia. Ultimately, it was taken over by William the Conqueror in his Norman Invasion of 1066.

The Norman Invasion is usually considered the beginning of England as it exists today. And not long after conquering England, the Normans turned west to Wales, but the Welsh fought them well. The crown eventually created a system in which the king set up castles where he could along the border between England and Wales, and installed lords in them. This created a complicated patchwork, where some parts of Wales were still basically independent principalities, while others answered to Marcher lords, nobles appointed by the king who ruled particular areas.

In the late 1200s, King Edward I managed to succeed where the Norman attempt had failed, conquering Wales. When he began his conquest in 1277, Llywelyn the Last (called Llywelyn ap Gruffudd in Welsh) had claimed the title "Prince of Wales," uniting most of the Welsh under his rule. After a six-year struggle, Edward's forces killed Llywelyn in battle and conquered his territory of

Gwynedd. To ensure English dominance, Edward placed more of Wales under royal control and set up more Marcher lords.

Some Welsh nobles were allowed to keep their lands, as long as they served as feudal lords under the king's influence. However, Edward made sure the general public understood who was in charge. He built new towns and new castles, adding a large military presence to the area. He also kicked many Welsh peasants out of their homes in the process, giving their land to English settlers.

Welsh folk tales of the time included stories about a hero who would lead the Welsh against this occupation and again establish Wales as a free and independent land. A few rebels tried during the 1300s, though they didn't have much success. When Owain Glyndwr arrived on the scene, he seemed to fit the bill.

Owain Glyndwr's early years don't suggest a man who would come to fight against English rule. Born in about 1354, he came from a wealthy, noble line, and was heir to Welsh estates on both sides of the family. He was educated in London, studying law there and marrying the daughter of one of the king's judges. He had even served the English cause as a young man, fighting for England against Scotland on behalf of King Richard II. Just days before he turned to rebellion in the year 1400, he was still a wealthy, upper-class Welsh noble, living in a mansion on a huge estate.

Some of the blame for Glyndwr's rebellion goes to King Henry IV, who in 1399 forced Richard II to give up the throne and sent the former king to his death. He imposed higher taxes on Wales, which, combined with an outbreak of the plague, made the Welsh population restless.

Blame also goes to a bad neighbor, Reginald de Grey, who served on King Henry's council and got Glyndwr in

Owain Glyndwr, as envisioned (literally) by William Blake.

trouble with the new king. To put it bluntly, Glyndwr and Grey didn't get along. For starters, Grey grabbed a piece of land Glyndwr owned, and the legal system took the Englishman's side. Then, when the king sent a summons for Glyndwr to report for army duty, Grey either deliberately didn't give him the message or (less likely) somehow forgot to do so.

As a result, Glyndwr didn't report in time or provide an advance reason why he would not. The king retaliated by declaring Glyndwr a traitor and an outlaw, and confiscating his land. This proved to be a step too far. Glyndwr organized a band of supporters who named him the new Prince of Wales on September 16, and he carried out an impressive first strike three days later—attacking and capturing Ruthin Castle, which was owned by Grey.

Over the next two years, his ever-growing Welsh army continued to attack English castles in what had historically been Welsh territory, driving the king's subjects from numerous towns in the northern part of Wales.

English attempts to quash the rebellion included a series of discriminatory laws passed in 1402, which banned Welshmen from holding certain offices, put limits on the education of Welsh children, and generally punished all of Wales for Glyndwr's insubordination. The upshot? They also generated more resentment toward England among the Welsh, leading more of them to join the revolution, with Welsh students and workers quitting their posts and turning into rebels.

By 1404, it looked like Glyndwr had achieved Welsh independence. Henry continued to send armies into Wales, but forces loyal to Glyndwr beat them back for most of the next decade, usually using guerrilla tactics to harass and surprise the English troops. One of the longest uprisings in the history of Britain, Owain Glyndwr's revolution was a rare success for the underdog.

Not just a military leader, the Prince of Wales also extended his revolution to establishing the institutions of a free Wales that could

THE PRINCE OF WALES

Though no Welshman since Glyndwr has held the title Prince of Wales, the designation still has its place in the British monarchy. Even before the English fully conquered Wales, the crown used the title to indicate who would be in charge next.

Starting with Edward II (born in Caernarfon, Wales), the title went to the eldest son of the king or queen of England, the presumed heir to the throne. Usually, the title gets passed down as soon as the current Prince of Wales becomes the king (or dies).

Under Queen Elizabeth II, her son Charles has held the title as the next in line for the throne (and he's gotten used to it, holding it for more than six decades).

AN ONGOING SEARCH

Glyndwr's final resting place remains a mystery. Adam of Usk, a contemporary of Glyndwr's, wrote in 1415 that Glyndwr died "after four years in hiding," was buried by his supporters, and was then reburied after the enemy found his grave. A mound near Monnington Court in Herefordshire often gets mentioned as Glyndwr's grave, though digs there haven't proven this. There's also the concept put forth in 1905 by Welsh nationalist Owen Rhoscomyl that Glyndwr's grave is in the heart of every true Welshman, and therefore will never be disturbed. Still, historians and archaeologists continue to look for clues about the last years of Glyndwr's life, keeping up interest in the Welsh hero in the process.

function as an independent nation. In 1404, Glyndwr organized a Welsh Parliament (which made his role as prince official), and began plans to create a separate church, two universities, and other institutions of a modern country. A charismatic leader and trained negotiator, Glyndwr also helped his cause by forming an alliance with England's other main enemy, France.

The rebellion began to fall apart in 1408, when England blockaded Wales to cut off supplies and then mounted a new invasion. Glyndwr's captured castles of Aberystwyth and Harlech were soon seized again by English forces. His wife and several of his children were captured in the latter attack, and all died prisoners in the Tower of London.

Without his land or his family, Glyndwr and some supporters turned into full-fledged guerrillas, constantly on the run. They continued to carry out raids against the king's armies for a few more years, but the chance for a free Wales was gone.

Owain Glyndwr disappeared from history around 1412—never captured or killed. Supposedly, he continued communicating with his supporters, though—when Henry died and was replaced by his son—many of them accepted the new king's offer of a pardon for turning themselves in and ending the war.

Individual Welshmen carried on attacks against English occupation after that, but never the kind of organized uprising tried under Owain Glyndwr, and never with anything approaching his success. In 1535 and 1542, the English Parliament passed the Laws in Wales Acts, which extended English legal and governmental systems to Wales—the last step in fully incorporating Wales into England's territory. ●

Joan of Arc: her sword belies her timid gaze.

JOAN OF ARC

THE TIME: *c. 1412–1431*

THE PLACE: *France*

THE OPPONENTS: *England, the Burgundians*

O ne of the most famous women of her day, Joan of Arc was a unique combination—a devout Catholic who claimed to talk to angels, a French warrior who took the fight to the opposition, and a teenage girl whose religious and military leadership (and martyrdom) still make her an iconic figure around the world.

When Joan was born, probably about 1412, she seemed an unlikely candidate for the kind of life she would eventually lead. Her parents were peasants in eastern France (d'Arc was probably a family name, not a hometown), and France wasn't in a terribly strong position. By the time of Joan's birth, France and England had already been engaged in a conflict for nearly eighty years, over who would hold the French throne.

What made Joan—whose birth name was actually Jehanne—unusual was her tendency to have visions. At the age of twelve, the deeply religious girl said she was visited by a trio of Catholic saints—Saint Michael (an archangel said to fight Satan in the Book of Revelations) and Saints Catherine and Margaret (in a bit of foreshadowing, both women who were martyred). They first appeared as voices, then as images. Joan claimed the saints told her to join the war, drive the English out of France, bring Charles VII to Reims, and install him as the king of France.

———

By this point, the Hundred Years' War between England and France had gone through several distinct phases. The most recent (often called the Lancastrian

Phase) began in 1415 when Henry V of England invaded France. In just a few years, Henry won the famous Battle of Agincourt, conquered most of Normandy, and cut a deal with the French king Charles VI that married Henry to Charles's daughter and made their future children (rather than the king's existing ones) the heirs to the throne.

Charles VI, by all accounts, was completely mad. For example, at various points he believed he was made entirely of glass and took extreme precautions not to shatter. So, he already had little control over state affairs, and his reign already included a war-within-a-war between the Burgundians (Frenchmen loyal to the Duke of Burgundy, who held Paris and Reims when Henry invaded) and the Armagnacs (who saw Charles VII as the rightful heir). The Burgundians made Charles VI sign the treaty with Henry and disown his own son.

When the mad king died in 1422 (shortly after Henry V's death), Charles VII declared himself king, while the English-Burgundian alliance declared Henry's infant son the king of France as well as of England. The sides continued to fight, and Joan's visions came a couple of years into that part of the conflict.

So, that was the complicated mess into which Joan of Arc entered on the instructions of her saintly visitors, with a goal of helping the underdog Charles reclaim the kingdom. Her first attempt at a military career didn't take. In 1428, Joan left her village and went to the town of Vacouleurs, where she asked the garrison for permission to visit the dauphin (the would-be king's title as heir) and his royal court. The sixteen-year-old girl with strange visions didn't impress the commander, but she chose to try again the following year.

The second time proved the charm. When she returned to Vacouleurs in the winter of 1429, Joan again explained that she was on what she considered a mission from God. Her prophet status got a boost in February, when she predicted an English victory outside of Orleans—one of the northernmost cities still loyal to the dauphin—and that battle's outcome proved her right a few days later. The garrison at Vacouleurs provided her with a few guards and Joan, disguised as a man, went to Chinon to see the future king.

After conducting the fifteenth-century equivalent of a background check to ensure she was sincere, Charles VII met with Joan and agreed to give her some troops to lead on his behalf. She turned down his offer of a sword, predicting she would find an ancient sword in an old cathedral. She did. She also predicted her efforts would force England to end the siege of Orleans. She was also right about that.

Orleans had already been under siege by English forces for about five months, with its defenders significantly outnumbered, when Joan and her troops showed up in the city on April 30. After the English army refused her call to

SAINT JOAN

On May 16, 1920, Joan of Arc received the highest honor the Catholic Church could provide, and was canonized as Saint Joan. Because she was excommunicated from the church, she first had to be found innocent, a process that actually happened fairly quickly. France retook Rouen in 1449, and French authorities conducted a posthumous investigation and appeal (held as a full courtroom trial) that cleared her name in 1456.

It took centuries for Joan to be considered not merely a wrongly convicted martyr but a Catholic saint. In 1909 at Notre Dame Cathedral in Paris, Joan was beatified, meaning the church considered her someone who could intervene on behalf of people who prayed in her name. Sainthood was the next step, and about 30,000 people showed up at St. Peter's Basilica in Rome for her canonization ceremony. Not surprisingly, she was also named the patron saint of France—as well as of soldiers.

withdraw, she rallied the defenders with her reputation for predictions and her aggressive approach to military strategy. Where other French commanders had been more focused on defense, Joan organized a series of quick offensive strikes. In the space of about a week, the defenders of Orleans drove away the English and captured their siege forts.

Her prediction of the victory, and her role in it, earned Joan the nickname "The Maid of Orleans." Despite her reputation as a military leader, Joan didn't fight in combat herself, and never personally killed an enemy soldier (though she did suffer injuries inflicted by archers, including one she'd allegedly predicted in advance). She was more of an inspirational figure and a strategist, and she was good in each of those roles.

Following what her visions had promised, Joan urged the dauphin to march on Reims as soon as possible and give his claim to the throne more legitimacy, by taking the city where French kings were traditionally crowned. Here again, she was more aggressive a leader than the French forces were used to, but she was making the right call. Joan helped lead an army north, winning victories along the way and surprising English commanders with the decision to skip attacking Paris and instead head straight to Reims.

On July 17, 1429, Joan of Arc achieved the goal her visions had set for her. The day after Reims opened its gates to the dauphin, he was crowned King Charles VII, and Joan took part in the ceremony.

That didn't end the war, though. In August, Joan helped lead an attack on Paris, where she was wounded by a crossbow, and the king eventually ordered

HEARING VOICES

Joan's reports of hearing and seeing what she considered messages from a higher power are a big part of her story. For many of those she led into battle, and to the Catholics who made her a saint, the voices and visions were miracles, proof of Joan's open line to her god. To modern researchers, they suggest she might have suffered from an illness of some kind. The non-divine explanations people have put forth over time include epilepsy, schizophrenia, a case of bovine tuberculosis . . . or just a made-up story.

his troops to retreat. Charles soon signed a truce with the Duke of Burgundy, but that peace proved very temporary and the armies were fighting again in less than a year.

When Joan took the field again in April, she did so as a noble, with her family line honored by the dauphin turned king. Her next campaign, though, ended tragically, just as she predicted in yet another vision. Joan was captured on May 23, 1430, leading an attack against a Burgundian force near the city of Compiegne, when she was pulled off her horse by an archer. The Burgundians turned her over to English troops for punishment.

Though she tried to escape several times, and though France launched several military campaigns toward Rouen while she was a prisoner, Joan was put on trial in January 1431 and convicted for heresy (based in part on her tendency to wear male clothing in battle). Originally, the English court at Rouen charged Joan with a slew of crimes—including everything from practicing witchcraft to stealing a horse—but the heresy charge was the eventual focus. The court proceedings were widely considered a sham at the time, and Joan proved an articulate witness in her defense, but the outcome was never in doubt. Joan of Arc was still only about nineteen years old when her English captors publicly burned her alive at the stake on May 30, 1431.

About five years after Joan's death, the Burgundians gave up on the war and agreed to recognize Charles VII as king. The Hundred Years' War didn't wrap up until 1453, when the English gave up and withdrew from France. To many, the retreat was a sign that Joan was right in predicting England would eventually be driven from the country. ●

MARTIN LUTHER

THE TIME: *1483–1546*

THE PLACE: *Germany*

THE OPPONENT: *The Catholic Church*

When a monk named Martin Luther raised his protests against the Catholic Church, the church was the most powerful institution in Europe, one that dominated both political and religious life. For better or worse, Luther's reform movement forever changed the long-held idea that there could only be one true Christian church, beginning a splintering process that's still ongoing.

Luther was born in Saxony, Germany, in 1483, when the territory was part of the Holy Roman Empire. Despite its name, the Holy Roman Empire was more of a loose coalition of European states than a true empire. When the actual Roman Empire collapsed in the west during the fifth century (the eastern part of the empire would remain intact for nearly a thousand more years, based in Constantinople and known as the Byzantine Empire), what followed was called the Dark Ages for good reason.

Western Europe was quite suddenly left without Roman-style education, technology, government, and commerce. And the only institution big enough to fill some of that vacuum was the Catholic Church. By the time of Luther's birth, the church had spent the better part of a millennium becoming the dominant force in much of Western Europe, spread both by war and by missionaries. Even the kings of Europe were careful not to cross the church.

The oldest child of a miner and smelter, Luther was educated in Latin and groomed for a career in law. His decision to instead become a monk was supposedly inspired by an experience traveling during a violent storm in July 1505, when he promised in prayer that he would join a monastery if he made it through his journey alive. He survived and kept his word, leaving law school to become

This portrait of Martin Luther appeared in his 1520 treatise On the Babylonian Captivity of the Church.

an Augustinian monk. Luther became an ordained priest in 1507 and in the winter of 1508–09 moved to Wittenberg, Germany, where he would become a doctoral student and teacher at the still-new and growing Wittenberg University.

While at the university, Luther took a trip to Rome for the first time, spending a few months in the heart of the Catholic world. Instead of impressing him, the trip reportedly soured Luther on some aspects of the church, as he saw what he considered corruption among some priests. He returned to Wittenberg still committed to his faith, but increasingly preached that faith alone could bring salvation—breaking with the church's position that charity and good works were just as important for an individual's "justification" in the eyes of heaven.

One particular kind of charity, the sale of indulgences, inspired the split that led to Luther's Protestant Reformation. In the Catholic doctrine of the time, it was believed that most dead souls had to spend time in purgatory before gaining entrance into heaven. Indulgences supposedly let the buyer bypass purgatory for heaven more quickly, solely in exchange for donating to the church on Earth. In 1517, Pope Leo X wanted to rebuild St. Peter's Basilica in Rome, and chose indulgences as a way to raise the money.

To Luther, it appeared that the already-wealthy church was enriching itself on the backs of believers, who felt pressured to pay so their departed friends and family could avoid long stints in purgatory. Luther also accused Johann Tetzel, a Catholic leader in Germany, of selling indulgences for sins that were not yet committed, thus opening a loophole that could be considered a free pass to commit any crime and get away with it in the eyes of the church—a loophole some figured out and exploited.

For Luther, indulgences were the last straw for what he saw as a thoroughly corrupt religious system. On October 31, 1517, Luther wrote a list of complaints about the practices of the church and nailed it to the door of the Wittenberg Cathedral. Writing, let alone publicly displaying, his *95 Theses on the Power and*

Efficacy of Indulgences was a gutsy move. Luther wasn't the first to criticize indulgences, but other opponents had been executed for doing so.

However, Luther garnered more popular support than previous church opponents. Within a few months, his friends and supporters had spread hundreds of printed copies of his theses throughout Germany, and soon thousands were circulating throughout Europe. He also had an important local supporter in Frederick the Wise, the Elector of Saxony, who protected Luther from arrest by papal authorities.

The Catholic Church had seen divisions before. The 1054 Great Schism divided the Catholic Church in the west and the Eastern Orthodox Church (a division that remains today), and the Great Western Schism in 1378 led to multiple popes with regional alliances before it was resolved in 1417. What made Luther and his movement different was he was dividing from the church completely, not forming a division within it. This became the Reformation—a reforming of church doctrine and practice—and that made Luther dangerous to both supporters and opponents.

So, in 1518, the church had Luther questioned on heresy charges in Augsburg, Germany. He refused to recant his theses, and publicly argued that the pope had no unique authority to interpret the Bible (another important point of Catholic doctrine at the time). Luther continued to teach his new take on the church, and on June 15, 1520, the pope issued a papal bull, warning Luther that he would be excommunicated if he didn't recant. He didn't, and was excommunicated on January 3, 1521.

Luther had to face secular authorities, too. A few weeks after his excommunication, he appeared at the unappealingly named Diet of Worms, an assembly of the Holy Roman Empire. Here, too, Luther was presented with his work and asked to recant it. Again he refused. On May 8, the Diet declared him a con-

STILL A WORLDWIDE PHENOMENON

The break Luther started still affects the religious world today. The Lutheran movement claims more than 75 million members around the world, with Germany (not surprisingly) the world leader in Lutherans, with more than 24 million. Lutheranism is also the official religion of the Church of Sweden, Church of Denmark, and Church of Norway, and has nearly four million followers in the United States. That's a lot of people. If you count all Protestants, there are something like 800 million people worldwide following the movement Luther began—including a majority of Americans. For his part, Luther never liked labels, always calling his followers simply "Christians."

START THE PRESSES

It's hard to overstate what a huge role the printing press played in creating the Reformation. Johannes Gutenberg invented the device in Germany about 1450, and even the earliest books were printed exponentially faster than by the former method of copying by hand. Because Luther's theses made up a fairly short document, his supporters were able to print them in pamphlet form far more quickly than a book and distribute them by the thousands, giving them away or selling them cheaply at a time when the high price and low supply of books made reading material hard for most people to come by.

victed heretic, making him a criminal under state law as well as church law and banning all his writings.

He escaped arrest on the way back to Wittenberg only because Frederick the Wise, in a pre-planned maneuver, sent men to intercept Luther and take him to Wartburg Castle for safe haven.

Arguably Luther's biggest contribution to religious practice came while he was lying low at Wartburg: his decision to translate the Bible from Latin into German. Prior to Luther's translation, most Christians couldn't read the Bible themselves, as Latin was a language reserved almost exclusively for study by priests and scholars. Having a Bible written in a vernacular language people actually spoke meant the general public could understand the book without relying on the interpretations of priests.

While Luther was away, Wittenberg became a hotbed for those who wanted even more dramatic change in the church. Luther returned to Wittenberg in 1522 and, somewhat ironically, became a conservative voice within the Reformation movement. Germany saw increasingly radical religious rebellions, including a series of armed revolts.

Instead of supporting these uprisings, Luther focused on building his new church. He wrote hymns, instituted a German-language mass, and developed other teachings that were a departure from Catholicism, though a more modest departure than some of the movements his rebellion spawned. He continued to write prolifically, establishing a number of church traditions (including a trend of virulent anti-Semitism and anti-Catholic teachings that unfortunately influenced Germany long after his death).

Rare for a church opponent of his time, Luther managed to avoid arrest his entire life, protected by his supporters as long as he stayed put. He spent the rest of his days in Germany, where he married a former nun and had a family (both radical acts for a former monk), dying of a heart attack in 1546 at the age of sixty-two. ●

GUY FAWKES

THE TIME: *1570–1605*

THE PLACE: *England*

THE OPPONENT: *Parliament*

Every year on November 5, the citizens of the United Kingdom set off fireworks and light bonfires, to celebrate the failure of a Catholic revolutionary who tried to blow up the seat of government. That foiled 1605 "Gunpowder Plot" made Guy Fawkes famous, and the foiling is still celebrated four centuries after his execution.

Though famous for his hatred of non-Catholics, Fawkes was actually born an Anglican in York in 1570. It's not entirely clear when or why he converted to Catholicism. It could have happened when his father died and his mother—whose own family was Catholic—married a Catholic man when Guy was eight years old. Or he may have converted when he attended a Catholic school in York, along with some other students who would later take part in the plan to blow up the government.

Either way, by the time he was twenty-one, he was both a true believer in Catholicism and a man jonesing to fight those who disagreed. Fawkes sold the home he'd inherited from his father and left England to join the Spanish army. Spain was already in the middle of fighting what would become known as the Eighty Years' War between Catholic Spain and the increasingly Protestant Netherlands.

Just fighting for Spain qualified as a revolutionary act, since England and Spain were still technically at war (even though they weren't actively fighting). Fawkes took it another step by campaigning to get the king of Spain to support an anti-Catholic rebellion in England to overthrow King James I. That attempt didn't succeed, and by 1604 Fawkes was back in his homeland and plotting other ways to revolt.

REMEMBER THIS

The date of Fawkes's attempt on the Parliament building is hard for the English to forget, especially because the Gunpowder Plot is commemorated with a famous and rather catchy poem. It begins:

> Remember, remember the fifth of November
> The gunpowder, treason and plot
> I know of no reason
> Why gunpowder treason
> Should ever be forgot.

The poem dates to at least 1870 (and possibly earlier), and goes on for quite a few more lines. Like most songs that have been around for such a lengthy period of time, it's gone through many versions, with most about eight verses long. Some suggest hanging the pope for his followers' crimes, while others merely insist "God save the King" (or Queen, as the case may be). They all start with the same opening line though, ensuring the day does get remembered, and all end with an emphatic "hip hip hooray."

He wasn't alone. The English Reformation, in which King Henry VIII split off the Church of England from the pope's authority (largely because he wanted to get divorced), had happened only a few generations ago, and was still a fresh wound to some Catholics in England. Though there was back-and-forth between the country's religious status under Henry's initial successors—Queen Elizabeth I and her replacement, King James—the Church of England became more Protestant and the government regularly persecuted Catholics. The crown treated loyalty to the pope as disloyalty to the country—and a sign of possible allegiance to Spain—and fined anyone who refused to attend a Protestant church.

In spite of the notoriety Fawkes received at the time (and now), he wasn't the one who actually led the Gunpowder Plot. Robert Catesby—like Fawkes, a former Protestant turned Catholic zealot—recruited and organized the conspirators. On May 20, 1604, the five key members of the conspiracy—Catesby, Fawkes, Thomas Percy, John Wright, and Thomas Wintour—met in a pub and outlined their plans together.

The idea was to kill the king and the members of Parliament in one fell swoop, decapitating the government and setting up a way to install Catholic leaders in head roles. Since he had experience with explosives, Fawkes took on the job of inciting the actual blast. Five days after the pub meeting, the conspirators bought the lease on an unused undercroft located right under the Palace of Westminster, where both houses of Parliament met. The large storage room was a perfect place to store explosives, and Fawkes started filling it with gunpowder.

The plot had a certain hapless quality, with lots going wrong along the way. Fawkes and the others wanted to blow up Parliament when it opened for session, but the session got pushed back to November 5 because of fears over a plague outbreak. The delay was long enough for some of the thirty-six barrels of gunpowder the plotters had already stored to go bad, forcing them to get more. There were also stories that, before buying the undercroft, the plotters had tried digging a tunnel under Parliament (probably untrue, as no tunnel was found).

Strangely, an act of selective compassion by one of Fawkes's associates was what alerted the authorities to what they were up to. One of the conspirators— or someone already familiar with the conspiracy—decided it would be unfair to blow up the Catholic members of Parliament along with the targets. On October 26, a Catholic member of the House of Lords, William Parker, received a letter warning him to avoid Parliament on the day of the planned attack. He showed the letter to the king, who took the threat seriously and sent an investigator to check out the cellars under the Parliament building the night before the bombing was supposed to occur.

The inspectors found Fawkes leaving the cellar, where he had worked that night to prepare for the next day's explosion, and found matches and a lantern on him. Of course, they also found a few dozen barrels of gunpowder, hidden under piles of wood and coal. When arrested, Fawkes gave a fake name (John Johnson) and a fake backstory with fake parents and a fake hometown, but he was honest about his goal: "to blow you Scotch beggars back to your native mountains."

Guy ponders gunpowder plots.

Fawkes was taken to the infamous Tower of London, where the king ordered increasing levels of torture until he gave up his co-conspirators. It took until November 6 just to get Fawkes to give authorities his real name, but the

BEHIND THE MASK

Fawkes, or at least a rough likeness of his face, made a comeback in the early days of the twenty-first century as a symbol of protest. The 2006 film *V for Vendetta*, based on a 1982 graphic novel of the same name, featured a mysterious revolutionary hiding behind a caricature of Fawkes (and plotting to blow up Parliament in the same manner Fawkes plotted against Parliament in his day).

In the aftermath of the financial crisis that caused the 2008 Great Recession in much of the world, that same mask became a popular choice for those wanting to broadcast their lack of satisfaction with powerful institutions. The masks became a uniform for the online hacker organization Anonymous, initially adopted during the group's 2008 protests against the Church of Scientology, and later used for all Anonymous activities. During the Occupy Wall Street protests that began in downtown New York before spreading throughout the United States, protesters regularly donned the Guy Fawkes mask. Wikileaks founder Julian Assange wore the same mask at an Occupy event at the London Stock Exchange, and protest movements in India, Canada, Poland, and elsewhere adopted the mask as well, making it so popular that the government of Saudi Arabia banned it. Protesters generally seemed to view Fawkes more as a general anti-establishment figure than the specifically religious-driven figure he always was.

torture eventually broke him and he named names. The king sent men after the other plotters. Some, including Catesby, holed up in a house in Staffordshire, where (in addition to accidentally starting a fire while trying to dry out some gunpowder) they were either killed or arrested.

Those arrested, including Fawkes, stood trial for high treason on January 27, 1606. There wasn't much chance of acquittal—the eight defendants made their pleas on a scaffold built just for the occasion. (Fawkes chose to plead not guilty, despite his earlier admission.)

Four days later, Fawkes and three of his co-conspirators were dragged along the ground by horses and brought to a scaffold directly across the street from the very building they'd tried to blow up. Fawkes managed to break his own neck on the scaffold, giving himself a quicker death than his co-conspirators, who were quartered alive—cut into four pieces—after being hanged just long enough not to die. Still, Fawkes's corpse was also quartered and sent to different spots in the kingdom to serve as a warning of what would happen to anyone conspiring against the crown.

The United Kingdom still celebrates the failure of the gunpowder plot every year on its anniversary, with a national holiday dubbed Guy Fawkes Day (also called Bonfire Night or Treason Night). The fireworks represent the gunpowder that didn't go off, and it's also tradition to burn effigy figures of Guy Fawkes (though, strangely, not of his partners in crime). •

OLIVER CROMWELL

THE TIME: *1599–1658*

THE PLACE: *England*

THE OPPONENT: *The English monarchy*

Before Oliver Cromwell, the power of the English monarchy was rarely questioned among the English themselves. There had been succession contests and battles, when it wasn't clear who was the rightful king or queen. But what Cromwell changed was the notion that there even had to be a monarch. By the time Cromwell was done, England would have royals again, but they would always have to acknowledge the power of Parliament.

Since the 1200s, Parliament had played an important role in governing the country, giving the king's subjects a chance to file grievances and promote laws through a democratic body. King James I had clashed with Parliament, but his son, Charles I, took that to another level. Only a particularly divisive king could turn Parliament into an open rebellion against him, but King Charles I proved that divisive. After a contentious session in 1628–29, he dissolved Parliament, locking its doors and refusing to let its members meet for eleven years.

It wasn't as if he was doing well without them, with England in financial ruin and the public angry over his draconian rule. Charles also tried imposing the English church system on the Scots, which prompted a war with Scotland that would become known as the Bishops' War. Fittingly, the war required Charles to raise money, and finally he had no choice but to recall Parliament in 1640, since only it had the power to raise the kind of revenue he needed.

Oliver Cromwell, born in 1599 to a modest member of the gentry, had taken a seat in Parliament for the first time in 1628. He returned when it met again,

Cromwell's dog is the smuggest dog in this satirical Dutch cartoon.

and soon became one of several important voices criticizing the king. Parliament moved quickly to impeach some of the king's top advisors, repeal laws the king imposed in its absence, and file grievances against the king's rule.

In 1642, tensions between the king and Parliament exploded into a civil war when Charles unsuccessfully sent troops to arrest five of his harshest critics in the House of Commons. With the failure of that unprecedented move, the king fled London and declared war on Parliament, and both sides began raising armies.

Cromwell took part in several of Parliament's military victories, including that in the 1644 Battle of Marston Moor, a crucial victory that gave Parliament control of the north of England. Cromwell earned higher ranks throughout the civil war, going from a man with little to no fighting experience to one of Parliament's best commanders. His military reputation was earned not just on the strength of his strategies and tactics, but thanks to his willingness to join the thick of battle. At a time when a leader taking the battlefield often meant commanding men from behind, Cromwell led by example and joined the front lines. He suffered his share of physical injuries, but he earned the loyalty of his soldiers in the process.

When Parliament passed a new law the following year that required members to choose whether to serve in the command of the army or in civil office (a way of making them better focus on the dual priorities of winning the war and running the country), Cromwell was the only member to choose the army. More than that, he helped create a new kind of army.

Replacing the old, hard-to-manage system of locally raised, ad hoc units based around garrisons, the New Model Army was instead a standing, centrally run force that could fight anywhere. Sir Thomas Fairfax was the army's general, but Cromwell was second in command and in charge of the cavalry, a group he called his "Ironsides." The New Model Army debuted in April of 1645 and won the war in less than a year. It crushed the main Royalist army at the Battle of Naseby in June and consistently defeated other Royalist forces, eventually forcing the deposed king to surrender.

———

SPARKING ANOTHER REBELLION

To the English, Cromwell was a revolutionary; to the Irish, he was the definition of an oppressor. Cromwell's invasion of Ireland was particularly brutal, as the zealous Puritan commander saw Irish Catholics as heretics and treated Irish Royalists with less regard than their English counterparts. His 1649 invasion included several extreme atrocities, starting with the Siege of Drogheda, where Cromwell's army massacred the town's full garrison (including priests and civilians) even after they surrendered. The brutality prompted a greater commitment to armed rebellion from the Irish and, in turn, fierce anti-guerilla tactics from the English.

The Drogheda massacre was only the start of a long campaign of destruction that also caused a massive famine throughout Ireland, as crops were burned and the population pushed west. As many as 600,000 people died, more than 40 percent of a total Irish population of about 1.4 million. It's not surprising that Cromwell remains a villain in Ireland, or that Irish musicians including the Pogues, Morrissey, and Flogging Molly have written songs that curse the name of Oliver Cromwell.

The king's 1646 arrest put Parliament in undisputed control of England, though it had to fight a second civil war against Royalist supporters, in which Cromwell again proved an effective military commander. Parliament then purged its membership in 1648, leaving only a "Rump Parliament" of hardline anti-Royalists (including Cromwell) in charge. The rebels turned rulers took the final step in 1649, sentencing the deposed king to death and executing the hereditary ruler of England for treason.

With the king dead, Parliament declared England a republic, establishing the Commonwealth of England in 1649. Cromwell spent more than two years on military campaigns on behalf of the Commonwealth, invading first Ireland and then Scotland. Those invasions established that Cromwell had a ruthless streak when it came to those who questioned him. He put down Royalist uprisings in both lands, with a high human cost.

After returning to England, he showed his ruthlessness again by essentially staging a military coup in 1653. After sitting through sessions that tried his patience, he considered the Rump Parliament ineffective, and he ordered soldiers loyal to him to clear the chamber. As Charles had decades earlier, Cromwell dissolved Parliament on his own authority; only he did so on authority he'd given himself.

A few months later, the new Parliament recruited by Cromwell instituted a temporary constitution called the Instrument of Government. This new system gave Cromwell the title of Lord Protector for life, the sole executive power above an army loyal to him and a Parliament that (though it had veto powers)

A WAR ON CHRISTMAS

English life under Cromwell was predictably puritanical in many ways, including the way people could celebrate the inspiration for Cromwell's religion. He had a reputation for banning Christmas, but that's not entirely true; instead, he banned most aspects of Christmas celebrations, restricting the holiday to a day of fasting and reflection—an austere holiday more in line with his strict beliefs than the fun family feast it had already become to many. Cromwell banned everything from cooked goose to holly, and even Christmas Mass. That didn't last, as Charles II repealed all of Cromwell's Christmas bans before his first holiday as king.

was nearly as loyal. At one point, Parliament offered to make Cromwell king of England; he weighed the decision for weeks before declining the crown. That didn't stop him from ruling like a king for his five years as Lord Protector. While he allowed a fair amount of religious tolerance, even letting Jews return to England after years in exile, he integrated Puritanism into state institutions, and went to war with Spain and the Netherlands partly for religious reasons.

———

In many ways, the Parliament's devolution into one-man rule actually convinced a chunk of England that the system needed a monarch. Cromwell and his fellow leaders in the civil war established a precedent that would give Parliament more say in the future, but the outcome undermined the idea of Parliament ruling without a king. While Cromwell's supporters still saw him as a revolutionary hero who helped overthrow a corrupt king, his enemies called him a usurper and a hypocrite who had become the same thing he once fought.

Cromwell died of an illness at age fifty-nine and, in another act that belied his years of opposition to royalty, his son, Richard, replaced him as Lord Protector. Richard Cromwell was a weak leader, with an economy in ruin and the military in open rebellion against him. He dissolved his Parliament in April 1659 and resigned his post on May 25.

The monarchy was reestablished in 1660, just two years after Oliver Cromwell died. The executed king's son, Charles II, was installed on the throne and the constitutional changes Cromwell had created were largely scrapped. The following year, on the anniversary of the previous king's execution, the body of Cromwell was dug up and publicly hanged for a day (along with the bodies of two of his partners in regicide) in a posthumous public "execution" ceremony. His head, cut from his body post-hanging, wasn't reburied until 1960. ●

METACOM

THE TIME: *c. 1639–1676*

THE PLACE: *Wampanoag territory*

THE OPPONENT: *English settlers*

In a story familiar to most American schoolchildren, the Pilgrim settlers of Massachusetts and the local Wampanoag tribe came together in a celebration of Thanksgiving in 1621. That peace lasted only a few decades, however, as a new generation of settlers pushed farther into Wampanoag territory, and the war chief Metacom tried to protect his land and people by leading a bloody uprising.

Before English settlers arrived in America, the Wampanoag territory included much of what's now Massachusetts and Rhode Island. Just a few years before the settlers arrived, however, they had suffered a massive disease outbreak (possibly smallpox or leptospirosis) that killed a large portion of the Wampanoag. They had also lost population to slavers, who visited the coast and captured Native Americans to sell abroad.

Though early relations between the Wampanoag and the Pilgrim settlers of Plymouth Colony were generally good, that changed as more English settlers—most of them Puritans—arrived in the area. The peace between the two sides lasted as long as Metacom's father, Massasoit, remained chief, but there were already warning signs by the time Metacom (also called Metacomet) was born, about 1639. And by the time Massasoit died, in around 1660, tensions were high.

Metacom became grand sachem (head chief of all Wampanoag, as well as chief of his specific tribe) in 1662, after the Plymouth Colony played a role in his brother

ENGLISH NAMES

It's not entirely clear how Metacom came to be known as Philip, other than that the name was bestowed on him by the court of the Plymouth Colony. It might have been an effort by his father to curry favor with the settlers by having both his sons take English names (Wamsutta was called Alexander). It also may have been Wamsutta's decision, prompted by the influence of his Christian-convert translator. Either way, Metacom went from being just Philip to King Philip when he replaced his brother as sachem.

Wamsutta's untimely death. The colony's court had summoned Wamsutta to appear, and sent a small military force to bring him in at gunpoint. Wamsutta died of an illness shortly after his questioning, prompting rumors that the English had killed him by poisoning, or at least indirectly caused his death while he was in their care.

The next decade produced plenty of other causes for the eventual war. Waves of Puritan settlers were taking over more and more land, extending well past the borders the Pilgrims had agreed to with Massasoit. As settlers became accustomed to their new land, they needed less help from the native peoples, and introduced commodities like alcohol that they could trade for more than what they were worth. The Wampanoag and others were also forced to sign treaties with the growing white colonies; in 1671, Metacom himself was ordered to sign a peace deal in the village of Taunton, in which he agreed for his people to hand over weapons to the colonists. Puritan religious leaders viewed the Native Americans as uncivilized, and made a point of converting as many as they could to Christianity, creating a class of "Praying Indians," while the rest of the native peoples feared for the loss of their own religious traditions.

The incident that sparked Metacom's rebellion against his neighbors was the June 1675 murder of a "Praying Indian" and translator named John Sassamon, who was suspected of informing the settlers about tribal activities. Sassamon had earlier told officials that Metacom's negotiations with other local tribes were actually preparations for an attack; Metacom denied these charges in court, but the rumors fueled fears of an uprising. After Sassamon's murder, the Plymouth Colony responded by trying and executing three Wampanoag warriors for the crime, and Metacom responded in turn with the kind of uprising that seemed inevitable by that point.

On June 24, Metacom ordered an attack on the town of Swansee, launching what immediately became open war, with the white settlers fighting the Wampanoag and their allies. The conflict was dubbed King Philip's War, after the name the English called Metacom, and it became the bloodiest per-capita war in American history, with a higher percentage of the population killed than even during the Civil War.

The band of Wampanoag that attacked Swansee killed several colonists and burned the town to the ground. Less than a week later, Plymouth formed an alliance with the nearby Massachusetts Bay Colony, and their combined troops destroyed the Wampanoag village at Mount Hope in Rhode Island. It became clear early that this would be a total war with no negotiated peace; the territorial goals of both sides meant victory required one to destroy the other and take its land.

The Wampanoag and their allies took an early advantage during the summer by attacking one town after another, including Dartmouth, Brookfield, Deerfield, and Lancaster. With England itself in the middle of a civil war and colonies outside New England sitting on the sidelines, the colonists mostly had to fend for themselves in terms of supplies and reinforcements.

By September, the Plymouth and Massachusetts Bay colonies had formed the New England Confederation with colonies in Connecticut and Rhode Island, and the confederation formally declared war on Metacom. The Native Americans continued to make major gains, ambushing and killing about fifty colonists near Hadley, Massachusetts, and in October burning down most of Springfield—one of the largest settlements in the area at the time.

More local peoples joined the conflict, with the Narragansett, Pocumtuck, and Nipmuck eventually taking up cause with Metacom and the Wampanoag. Groups of Pequot, Mohegan, and Nauset sided with the colonists, as did the villages of "Praying Indians" established during the Puritans' conversion efforts.

Under Metacom's direction, the Wampanoag attacked Plymouth Plantation itself in March 1676—proving they could reach even the best-fortified colonial towns—and burned down the city of Providence. Metacom's forces completely destroyed a dozen towns in New England during the war, and killed somewhere between 5 and 10 percent of the colonial population.

Metacom, standing at a cultural crossroads.

Metacom's success, however, was short-lived. By April of 1676, the colonists had managed to defeat the Narragansett and kill their chief, costing Metacom a crucial ally. The Native American troops were running low on ammunition and supplies, and Metacom's attempts to make alliances with French colonies and Iroquois nations didn't work out. The colonies also decided to offer amnesty to Native Americans who surrendered, costing Metacom hundreds of troops by early summer.

With his war falling apart, Metacom fled Massachusetts, and the colonists sent raiding parties to search for him. On August 12, 1676, he was assassinated by a Wampanoag soldier named John Alderman, who had converted to Christianity and joined the colonists' cause. The Wampanoag chief had been hiding in a swamp in Rhode Island, but his whereabouts were betrayed to the Puritans. Metacom's corpse was drawn and quartered, and his head was paraded around the colony on a stick, kept on display for twenty years. His only son was shipped to Bermuda as a slave, along with other captured Wampanoag.

Killing Metacom basically ended the uprising, since the Wampanoag forces couldn't hold out much longer. Some survivors escaped to Canada, while others were captured and sold into slavery. As few as 400 Wampanoag survived the two-year conflict, and their allies, including the Narragansett and the Nipmuck, were similarly devastated by the end. About 2,000 Wampanoag survive today, mostly in the same part of the country for which their ancestors fought. Their numbers are split between two federally recognized tribes, many living on a reservation on the island of Martha's Vineyard.

As for the colonists, their defeat of Metacom proved costly at the time, but their victory gave them land and room to grow. It also got the attention of the home country. England began to see more potential in the region and sent more colonists, establishing a pattern that would lead to centuries of tension and warfare between English settlers and Native American peoples across the continent. ●

SAMUEL ADAMS

THE TIME: *1722–1803*

THE PLACE: *United States*

THE OPPONENT: *Great Britain*

Thirteen colonies fought for independence, but the American Revolution really got its start in Massachusetts. Long before most of the nation's founding fathers had plans to rebel, rebels in Boston were taking to the streets to protest British rule. Many early events involved Samuel Adams, and the Boston leader earned his nickname as "the father of the American Revolution."

Adams was born September 27, 1722, in Boston, the son of a business owner and local politician. He certainly had brains; he enrolled at Harvard at age fourteen. He also had an interest in politics, an enthusiasm at least partially inspired by his father's experiences with the British government.

Samuel's father, Deacon, along with other members of the Boston Caucus political party, started a "land bank" that loaned citizens money borrowed against their mortgages. The British government opposed this move and shut down the bank. Deacon Adams was among those held responsible for paying the bank's debts when it suddenly closed—debts that stayed with the family well after Deacon died and Samuel inherited his estate.

The break between the American colonies and their overseas government owed a lot to the perceived unfairness of British taxation policies. Tensions escalated after Britain and the colonies won the Seven Years' War (called the French and Indian War by colonists) in 1763. Britain had amassed a major war debt, in a war it saw as benefitting the colonists at least as much as the home country, and started taxing the colonies as a way of paying it down. Samuel Adams was

BREWING UP

A whole generation also knows Samuel Adams as a brewer, thanks to a beer that shares his name. In the 1980s, the Boston Beer Company dubbed its flagship line Samuel Adams, with its logo showing the revolutionary leader holding a stein and identified as "Brewer. Patriot." The irony is that, while Adams worked as a partner in his father's malt house after failing at his own business, he wasn't very successful as a brewer.

one of many future Americans who had a problem with this idea of taxation by Parliament without representation in Parliament, and he did what he could to oppose it.

One of the first ways Great Britain tried to pay its war debts with colonial money involved passing the controversial 1764 Sugar Act, which added duties on sugar and other imported goods. The following year came the Stamp Act, which Adams considered even worse. The law required most kinds of paper goods sold—anything from legal contracts to newspapers to decks of playing cards—to carry a stamp, making the tax hard to avoid. The Stamp Act created real opposition in America, with nine colonies forming a "Stamp Act Congress." The body wrote the king to argue that, despite being loyal subjects, colonists felt only colonial governments could pass a tax like the Stamp Act. The Boston opposition was less polite.

In 1765, Adams—along with John Hancock—founded a secret protest group called the Sons of Liberty, which organized street protests. In one memorable display, the group organized a mob to hang and behead an effigy of Andrew Oliver, the local stamp distributor. The Sons of Liberty also trashed his home, and Oliver quickly resigned. The intimidation factor worked, with enough similar protests in other towns—and enough stamp distributors resigning in fear— that the Stamp Act was repealed the year after it debuted.

———————

Still in need of money, the British government wasn't going to give up that easily. Starting in 1767, it passed the Townshend Acts, a series of laws designed to show the colonies who was in charge. One of them, the Revenue Act, gave a lot more power to British customs officials in the colonies, which was extremely unpopular in a port city like Boston. Customs officials seizing a boat owned by John Hancock (ironically named the *Liberty*) and putting a Sons of Liberty leader on trial for smuggling didn't help matters, even though Hancock was eventually acquitted. Adams (at this time a member of the state legislature) responded to the Townshend Acts by organizing an effective boycott of British imports, reaching out to other colonies and trying to get them to join in.

By the fall of 1768, Boston was under full military occupation, with Britain sending regiments of soldiers to enforce order on its subjects. On March 5, 1770, soldiers opened fire and killed five people in what became known as the Boston Massacre, considered by many the first shots fired in the American Revolution. Though the most violent clash so far, the Boston Massacre actually calmed things down, at least for a time. Seeing how far tensions had escalated, the British government repealed most of the Townshend Acts and lifted the occupation of Boston. This action ended up making Samuel Adams and his allies less influential, with their boycott of British goods less effective and Adams receiving less political support than before, despite winning re-election to the legislature.

But the temporary peace ended in 1773, when Parliament passed the Tea Act. This law wasn't a tax increase; it was a bailout of the East India Company, a major trading institution with huge debt and huge amounts of tea it couldn't sell. The Tea Act let the company sell tea outside of Britain directly, without using importers, and gave it a monopoly on the tea trade in the American colonies. While the Tea Act actually *lowered* the price of tea sold in America, it spurred a new round of opposition from merchants hurt by the monopoly and political leaders like Samuel Adams who saw it as a sneaky way of reestablishing Britain's right to dictate policy to the colonies.

That opposition culminated in the Boston Tea Party, one of the iconic events of the American Revolution and one that Adams helped organize. Dressed as Native Americans, members of the Sons of Liberty snuck onto the East India Company's boats and dumped 342 chests of tea into Boston Harbor on the night of December 16, 1773.

In response to the Boston Tea Party, Parliament passed a series of laws called the Coercive Acts that—among other punishments—closed the port of Boston, gave the king direct control over who could serve in the state government of Massachusetts,

Samuel Adams, Esquire, in an engraving from 1780.

COUSIN JOHN'S REVOLUTION

While Samuel Adams was the clear rabble-rouser of the family, his second cousin, John, was no slouch in the revolutionary department. Where Samuel was more likely to take to the streets, future president John was more likely to write a strongly worded letter. During opposition to the Stamp Act, he wrote a compelling defense of the colonists' position, and followed that up with a treatise attacking the idea that Parliament should be the main source of law in the colonies. Of course, when elected to the First Continental Congress, John Adams was on the five-man committee that put together the Declaration of Independence and got the revolution rolling.

and ordered all the colonies to provide housing for British soldiers. For Adams, this was further proof that he had been right to oppose the British policies all along, and more Bostonians than ever agreed.

The thirteen colonies responded to these laws (which they called the Intolerable Acts) by forming the First Continental Congress in 1774, and Adams was an obvious choice to serve as one of its representatives. When the Second Continental Congress met the next year to declare independence, Adams became a kind of elder statesman of the new revolution. He remained a member of the upstart congress through 1781, helping organize the colony-wide revolt in various administrative positions.

After the war was won and the Constitution was adopted, Adams continued his political career at the state level instead of the new federal one. In 1789, he was elected lieutenant governor of Massachusetts, with his former protégé John Hancock as governor. After four years, Adams became governor, and served one four-year term before retiring.

By the time Samuel Adams died at age eighty-one on October 2, 1803, he'd lived through the administrations of the first two presidents of the United States (the second being his cousin, John), and had seen the revolution he helped spark lead to a stable and growing nation. ●

GEORGE WASHINGTON

THE TIME: *1732–1799*

THE PLACE: *United States*

THE OPPONENT: *Great Britain*

George Washington boasted a résumé few revolutionaries could hope to top, serving as his country's first president and presiding over the creation of its constitution. Before all that could happen, though, the United States had to win its war against Great Britain, and that's where Washington really established his bona fides.

Washington was born in 1732, the son of a successful plantation owner whose family had come to Virginia from England in the mid-1600s. When he was eleven his father died, preventing George from getting the European education common for boys of his circumstances.

Instead, at sixteen George Washington began a career as a surveyor, learning the landscape of Virginia. In 1752, his half-brother died, and twenty-year-old George inherited his estate and plantation at Mount Vernon. But he didn't have long to settle in before a new career came calling.

Washington's military career began while serving for Great Britain in the French and Indian War (the North American component of the Seven Years' War between Britain and France). In October 1753, the British governor of Virginia sent Washington to order the French off a piece of disputed land. France, predictably, refused. Washington's troops later surprised a French outpost and killed its commander, but Washington was soon surrounded and forced to surrender.

Despite that failure, he got another chance. Washington later served as a colonel under General Edward Braddock, survived the ambush that killed the

George Washington: tight in tights.

general (despite being shot and having a horse shot out from under him), and was appointed commander of all Virginia troops at the young age of twenty-three.

When the war ended in Virginia in 1758 (Britain won the whole thing in 1763), Washington resigned his commission and headed back to Mount Vernon. He got married, was elected to the Virginia legislature (the House of Burgesses), and began to devote his life to farming. He quadrupled the size of Mount Vernon, growing a variety of crops (and owning a large number of slaves, as he would his entire life; only in his will did he free the people who actually worked his land).

NOBLE ROMAN

Washington's decision to willingly turn down a lifetime of power earned him the nickname "The American Cincinnatus," a high compliment among people who saw Rome as an inspiration. Cincinnatus was a former Roman consul who in 458 BCE (and again in 439) was called out of retirement by the Senate and appointed dictator—an all-powerful position Rome only filled during a worst-case scenario. Both times, he led Rome through the crisis and then voluntarily resigned the post and returned to his farm—supposedly literally beating his sword into a plowshare. When Washington willingly walked away from the presidency, Americans readily drew a parallel between the two powerful men.

It was the debt Britain acquired with its war victory that caused the very revenue-generating policies that eventually pushed the colonies toward revolution, and it was those policies that drew Washington back into a military uniform.

By the time colonial leaders were considering declaring independence, Washington had become an opponent of many British policies. He disliked the Stamp Act, and really hated the Townshend Acts. He tried to persuade the House of Burgesses to boycott British goods, and was among those calling for a colonies-wide assembly to stand up to Britain. In 1774, Washington was elected as one of Virginia's representatives to the First Continental Congress, which met to protest its grievances to the British government.

By the time the Second Continental Congress met in May 1775, colonial militias had fought British troops at Lexington and Concord, and the congress decided it needed to form the colonial militias into a Continental Army in order to fight a real war. By colonial standards, Washington was a veteran commander, and on June 14 he was appointed general of the new army.

Washington understood that his mostly untrained and poorly equipped force was a huge underdog against one of the best militaries in the Western world (even though Britain sent a fairly small force in its fight against the colonies). He decided on a strategy of avoiding the British in open-field battle whenever

A STERN WARNING

In his farewell address as president in 1796, Washington issued a series of pre-scient warnings about the country's future. He warned about the dangers of sectionalism, a problem that eventually led to the Civil War. He warned about permanent alliances overseas, which the United States managed to avoid until it formed NATO in 1949, ramping up the Cold War. He also warned that political parties would divide the country, which started happening as soon as Washington announced he wasn't seeking a third term.

possible, instead harassing their forces and using his familiarity with the terrain to his advantage.

While Washington and his men managed to drive British occupiers out of Boston in March 1776, other early battles didn't go well. The Continental Army lost a series of clashes in New York against British troops led by William Howe. In November, Washington was unable to hold New York City against Howe, with nearly 3,000 of his men surrendering and the rest fleeing with him across the Delaware River.

Defeat seemed likely at several points during the eight years Washington fought the revolution, particularly during the harsh winter of 1777–78, which he and his men spent freezing in Valley Forge, Pennsylvania, with thousands dying. Relief came via some powerful alliances with Britain's rivals—particularly France, which sent troops and experienced commanders like the Marquis de Lafayette to help Washington's cause.

Washington's masterstroke as a general came in 1781. For years, he had focused his efforts on keeping the British army in New York from advancing, but was unable to reclaim the city from Howe. With that strategy stuck in a holding pattern, he decided to instead move his men down to Virginia and defeat the British force based in Yorktown and led by Charles Cornwallis.

Bringing a combination colonial and French force to Yorktown, Washington put the city under siege, while French ships surrounded it by sea. The tactic worked in less than a month, and on October 19, 1781, Cornwallis surrendered to Washington. Only one British commander was conceding a loss, but the surrender of more than 8,000 troops at Yorktown proved sufficiently decisive that Britain agreed to negotiate an end to the war. In April 1782, the colonies sent a team of negotiators—Benjamin Franklin, John Adams, John Jay, and Henry Laurens—to Paris to work out an agreement with Great Britain. On September 3, 1783, the Treaty of Paris made the end of the revolution—and the creation of the United States of America—official.

When the war ended, Washington again tried to leave public life and quietly farm his plantation. And again, after a few years, he was dragged back by a crisis.

The weak post-revolution federal government created by the Articles of Confederation didn't take long to prove a failure. The states were all deeply in debt, Congress was handcuffed by its limited power, and it looked like the new nation might not last long. Washington was among those who thought the United States needed a convention to rewrite the Articles and produce a stronger government.

The delegates to the 1787 Constitutional Convention unanimously elected Washington to oversee it, and the group toiled through the summer to produce the Constitution that has served as the country's governing system for more than two centuries. His success at keeping order as the Constitutional Convention settled its complicated disputes made George Washington a logical choice for the newly created office of president. In 1788, the also-new Electoral College unanimously chose Washington for a four-year term as chief executive.

As the first executive power of a new country, Washington was extremely careful about precedent, since his every act was by definition historic. He put together an all-star team of advisors, installing political rivals like Thomas Jefferson and Alexander Hamilton in key roles so he could get their competing perspectives. He rebuilt the economy, kept the country neutral when France and Great Britain again went to war, expanded the country's boundaries west, and generally laid the foundation for what the United States would become.

Washington could have been even more powerful than he was, and his decisions to turn down that power added to his reputation. Having rejected a chance to be king right after the revolution, he avoided any royal trappings while in office, and turned down a third term as president.

He finally retired to Mount Vernon after eight years in office, when his vice president, John Adams, became president after defeating Thomas Jefferson (see page 87) in the country's first contested election. His retirement lasted less than three years, as Washington died at sixty-seven of a throat infection on December 14, 1799. ●

TOUSSAINT LOUVERTURE

THE TIME: *c. 1743–1803*

THE PLACE: *Saint-Domingue*

THE OPPONENT: *Slavery*

Toussaint Louverture pulled off a feat no other revolutionary leader can claim. Not only did he lead a slave revolt that successfully ended slavery in his homeland, but in Haiti he also produced the only modern nation created by a slave uprising.

Louverture was born into slavery in the early 1740s, in what was then the French territory of Saint-Domingue. France had taken over the western half of the island of Hispaniola from Spain in 1659 and established a colony based on large slave plantations. (Spain still controlled the eastern half of the island, which is now the Dominican Republic.) The colony quickly became a valuable outpost for France, a source of sugar cane, refined sugar, indigo, cotton, and coffee. It also became a massive hub for the transatlantic slave trade; by the 1780s, it accounted for about one third of that trade.

Originally called Toussaint Breda, after the name of the Breda plantation where he was born, Toussaint was granted his freedom by 1776—his age was listed as thirty-three on the paperwork—but continued to work on his old plantation as an employee, including as an overseer of his former master's slaves. By the time the Saint-Domingue revolution started, he had rented his own small coffee plantation and become a solidly middle-class landowner.

Toussaint's situation wasn't all that unusual; the island had a significant number of free black citizens, some of them freed slaves and others mixed-race offspring of white colonists and African slaves. Though quite a few of them owned land—and blacks outnumbered whites in Saint-Domingue by about ten to one—the island's laws still gave preferential treatment to the white colonists. People of color were barred from certain jobs and social events, and weren't allowed to carry weapons.

When the people of France overthrew their own government in the name of liberty and equality in 1789 (see page 97), French citizens of Saint-Domingue (and the island's slaves, too) felt those same ideals should apply to their situation.

The French Revolution gave the slaves of Saint-Domingue a perfect opportunity to rebel. Not only did the French passage of the Declaration of the Rights of Man give them a strong philosophical argument for freedom, but France was far too focused on its internal affairs to play much of a role in policing its colonies. In 1791, a slave uprising began in the north of Saint-Domingue, the first actions of a struggle that would last more than a decade and involve a strange mix of shifting alliances. Within a month, more than 1,000 plantations were burned or destroyed, and hundreds had been killed.

Toussaint first helped the overseers of the Breda plantation and their families escape the island, before turning his attention to aiding the rebels as a medic. Early on, however, he showed his skills as a leader and a tactician, and he soon became the general of the slave forces. He had a knack for diplomacy, too, convincing the Spanish to send the slaves much-needed supplies.

The next few years saw alliances shift constantly on the island. At first, white colonists and free blacks tended to side together against the slave rebels, while some in that coalition also wanted independence from France. The entry of Spanish aid into the conflict made free blacks more loyal to France, since the revolutionary government seemed to support equality (at least for free people), while Spain definitely did not. Things got even more complicated when the new French republic declared war on both Spain and Great Britain, and both those countries invaded Saint-Domingue.

With his success both in battle and in gaining supporters, Louverture—the last name Toussaint had taken by this point (see sidebar, page 86)—also changed his goals. Where the slaves had originally fought simply for better conditions, by 1793 the revolution was focused on ending slavery entirely.

The French republic's main civil commissioner in the colony, Léger-Félicité Sonthonax, promised freedom to any slaves who would support France in battle against the Spanish and British. On August 29, 1793, Sonthonax went a step further and abolished slavery in the north of Saint-Domingue, and his fellow commissioners in the colony soon followed his lead.

Louverture was skeptical of Sonthonax's promise at first, and most of the former slaves were slow to switch allegiances. But once the government in Paris announced an official end to slavery, in February 1794, Louverture and his men sided with France as free French citizens.

———————

Louverture's army of former slaves proved invaluable to France, driving pro-Spanish forces out of Saint-Domingue and containing the British in their base on the western part of the island. By 1797, Louverture had those foreign threats under control, had survived an attempt by another commander to split his forces, and had earned official French appointment as the colony's top military commander and its lieutenant governor.

With his military and popular support, he was now the de facto ruler of Saint-Domingue. Louverture wasn't concerned with making the colony independent; he just wanted its people to enjoy the same rights and freedoms as all other Frenchmen. So, as long as France supported the abolition of slavery, he avoided any attempt to declare independence.

By early 1801, Louverture had invaded the Spanish colony of Santo Domingo, freeing the slaves there as he conquered territory. That same year, he declared himself governor-general for life, and on July 7 he proclaimed a new constitution for all of Hispaniola—a constitution that stated, "All men are born, live and die free and French."

Louverture tried to get Napoleon Bonaparte—who had taken power in a coup against the French republic in 1799—to recognize his 1801 Constitution. Napoleon, however, didn't accept the idea of a colony telling him what it thought he should do. He also intended to reinstate slavery (though he kept that a se-

ORIGIN OF LOUVERTURE

While it's well known that Toussaint chose the surname Louverture in the early 1790s, no one is quite sure why. It's French for "the opening," but beyond that, it's unclear. One theory is that it referenced his tactical ability to create openings for his forces in battle. Another posits that the name was a reference to a gap in his teeth, caused by a musket ball. Though these days his name is often written "L'Ouverture," which is the preferred French spelling, he never used the apostrophe in his own writing.

cret at first). He sent a force of about 20,000 troops to Saint-Domingue, under the command of his brother-in-law, Charles Leclerc, who arrived in January 1802. Though the French arrivals first tried taking power by diplomacy, the fighting that followed was particularly rough. French troops also suffered massive casualties from an outbreak of yellow fever, while the island's defenders burned supplies and land to keep them out of French hands.

On May 6, Louverture and Leclerc agreed to a ceasefire, and the aged Haitian general retired to his plantation. Unfortunately for Louverture, French authorities still feared his power, and wanted him arrested. He was invited to a meeting by a French general, which was presented as a

A nineteenth-century engraving of a very dapper Toussaint Louverture.

friendly discussion but was a trap from the beginning, and ended with Louverture being placed under arrest and deported to France. There, he was locked away without trial and tortured for information. Toussaint Louverture died of pneumonia in the Fort-de-Joux prison in eastern France on April 7, 1803.

During his deportation, Louverture had declared, "In overthrowing me you have cut down in Saint-Domingue only the trunk of the tree of liberty; it will spring up again from its roots, for they are many and they are deep." In this case, those roots were many and deep enough to finish the job.

The fight for Haitian independence ended a few months after Louverture's death, with the Battle of Vertières on November 18, 1803. Haitian forces defeated the last major French stronghold, whose commander surrendered and agreed to return his few thousand remaining men to France in just a few days. On January 1, 1804, revolutionary leaders declared an independent Republic of Haiti, with Louverture's top lieutenant commander, Jean-Jacques Dessalines, as its first head of state. ●

THOMAS JEFFERSON

THE TIME: *1743–1826*

THE PLACE: *United States*

THE OPPONENT: *Great Britain*

Thomas Jefferson never fought in a battle during the Revolutionary War. He wasn't an exciting speaker who roused people to action, or a charismatic leader who worked the crowd. What he contributed to the revolution was a set of powerful ideas, and a way with words that still makes him highly quotable more than two centuries later.

Jefferson was born on a Virginia plantation in 1743, near the western border of the colony. He came from a wealthy family with a lot of land (and a lot of slaves), and as a boy he was an ambitious student. Besides farming, his father worked as a surveyor—he was the first man to complete a full map of Virginia—and collected a famously vast library for his day. Thomas Jefferson studied languages (he spoke five fluently) and supplemented his formal education by teaching himself from his father's books.

He graduated from the College of William and Mary in 1762, and went on to study law while still a teenager. When he turned twenty-one, he took ownership of his inheritance, including the land where he designed and built his Monticello estate, as architectural design was among the myriad skills he taught himself from his ever-expanding library.

After serving in a series of roles in local government and establishing himself as a prominent young lawyer, Jefferson—still only twenty-five—won election to the House of Burgesses (the Virginia legislature) in 1768. He was a poor public speaker, but his words gained authority when he committed them to paper. Jefferson was not only a remarkable writer, but one whose politics were more radical than most of his legislative colleagues. Jefferson particularly opposed British policies like the Townshend Acts and Intolerable Acts (see page 78), and befriended the bloc of legislators most opposed to them—a group that included George Washington (see page 79) and Patrick Henry.

When the First Continental Congress was announced, Jefferson drafted *A Summary View of the Rights of British America*, a pamphlet he gave the Virginia delegates in the hopes they would adopt it. They didn't (finding it too radical), but Jefferson laid out a compelling case that the colonies were already independent and that any laws Parliament imposed without colonial consent were therefore automatically illegal. It reflected Jefferson's belief in ideas like individual rights and self-determination, which had become popular causes in Europe among the Enlightenment thinkers of the time.

The pamphlet helped establish Jefferson as an important revolutionary voice and a skilled writer, and Virginia chose him as one of its delegates to the Second Continental Congress. The revolution had already started when the body met in May 1775, and the session's appeals to King George III didn't change anything. It became clear to the delegates that a full break with the home country was the only solution.

One of the congress's tasks then became to tell Great Britain that this was officially a revolution by people who demanded independence, not just a protest movement. To do that, the delegates decided to issue a formal declaration to inform the king and Parliament—as well as people throughout the colonies who would need to support and fight for independence—why the colonies wanted independence. The creation of the declaration was assigned to a committee with four other members—Benjamin Franklin, John Adams, Roger Sherman, and Robert Livingston—but Jefferson wrote the actual first draft.

It took just seventeen days in June 1776 (including a round of edits from other committee members) for Jefferson to produce one of the most important revolutionary documents

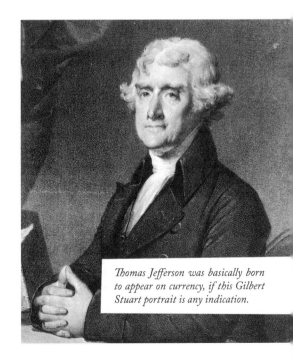

Thomas Jefferson was basically born to appear on currency, if this Gilbert Stuart portrait is any indication.

A HUGE CONTRADICTION

Like many of the founding fathers who hailed from the South, Jefferson's belief in people's rights came with an enormous contradiction—the fact that he owned other people as slaves. Though he consistently expressed opposition to the slave trade (his first draft of the Declaration of Independence called it "a cruel war against human nature itself"), he continued to own slaves, and built Monticello with slave labor. As president, he signed a law banning the transatlantic slave trade, but even that did nothing to diminish slavery within the United States, and Jefferson did not prevent slavery from spreading into newly acquired territories. Unlike George Washington, he didn't even free all his slaves when he died, only a few named individually in his will.

in world history. Among other things, he basically created a thesis statement for American democracy, with lines like: "We hold these truths to be self-evident, that all men are created equal, that they are endowed by their Creator with certain unalienable Rights, that among these are Life, Liberty and the pursuit of Happiness."

Things moved quickly from there. On June 28, Jefferson and his committee presented the Declaration of Independence to the delegates. Four days later, the Continental Congress voted to actually declare independence. In another two days, it approved a final version of Jefferson's declaration and printed copies to spread around the thirteen colonies.

Of course, the colonies won their independence from Britain through victory in the Revolutionary War. During that time, Jefferson shifted his focus back to Virginia politics, first as a legislator and then, in 1779, as governor. In the latter job, he wrote the Virginia Statute for Religious Freedom, which established the idea that "a wall of separation" should exist between affairs of church and affairs of state—another then-radical idea that would become a key part of American history.

Once the revolution against Great Britain was complete, Jefferson shifted roles and became a revolutionary voice within the new United States government.

Though the Articles of Confederation proved too weak to govern the country effectively, Jefferson opposed the idea of creating a new constitution. He feared that too strong a central government would lead to the same problems the colonies had faced under British rule, and that the proposed office of president could create a king in reality, even if not in title.

But he had little say in the matter, as the Constitutional Convention met in 1787 while Jefferson was overseas serving as America's minister in France (he'd taken the job over from Benjamin Franklin in May 1785). By the time Jefferson returned to America in September 1789, the Constitution had been the law of the land for more than six months.

Although it was created in his absence, Jefferson still found a way to affect the new Constitution. He corresponded with his friend James Madison, and together they created ten amendments to the new document. This Bill of Rights defined individual rights that had come under threat during British rule, from a separation of church and state to freedom of speech to the right to a fair trial. The amendments were ratified, making the constitution a far more democratic document.

Jefferson took the job of secretary of state in the presidential administration of his friend George Washington, and urged Washington to run for re-election after his first term. While Washington was able to generally unite the country during its crucial early years, political parties already began to form on his watch. John Adams and Alexander Hamilton became the faces of the Federalist Party, with Jefferson and Madison the leading figures in the Democratic-Republican Party (simply called the Republican Party at the time, it had little to do with the modern-day Republican Party).

Where the Federalists favored Britain in foreign affairs, Jefferson's party preferred France. The Federalists wanted more power centralized in the national government, while Jefferson's party favored the individual states. When Washington announced he would step down after two terms, Jefferson became the obvious choice to represent his party in the 1796 presidential election against the Federalist Adams (though he lost that vote).

Jefferson's victory against the sitting president Adams four years later is sometimes called the Revolution of 1800. And his election was a radical act at the time, one that showed the still-young country and its still-young system of government could handle transfers of power to an opposition party without descending into war. In his two terms as president, Jefferson significantly cut the national debt, won a war against pirates from the Barbary Coast of Africa, and purchased the Louisiana Territory from France—greatly expanding the size of the United States for about four cents per acre.

Still young during the revolution, Thomas Jefferson outlived most of the other founding fathers. He died at Monticello at age eighty-three, on July 4, 1826—the fiftieth anniversary of the Declaration of Independence. Not only that, he died just hours before his regular pen pal John Adams (whose last words were reportedly "Jefferson survives," as he hadn't heard the news). The stone on his Monticello grave doesn't even mention his presidency; at his insistence, it names only the achievements he saw as things he gave to the people—the Declaration of Independence, the Virginia Statute, and his post-presidential founding of the University of Virginia. •

DANIEL SHAYS

THE TIME: *1747–1825*

THE PLACE: *United States*

THE OPPONENT: *Taxes*

A variety of causes prompt revolts and revolutions, from wanting to liberate one's people to getting revenge on an invader to fighting for equality. Sometimes, though, it can be as simple as feeling ripped off financially. In the case of Daniel Shays, missing out on money he felt owed drove him into open rebellion, in the process causing the government of the new United States to realize it still had a lot to figure out in terms of running a country.

Born in Massachusetts in 1747, the child of Irish immigrants, Daniel Shays worked mostly as a hired laborer on others' farms. While working in Brookfield, Massachusetts, he also helped train a local militia and showed a knack for military-style drilling. That became a valuable skill once his home state became ground zero for the colonial revolution against the British.

Shays was an early volunteer to the revolutionary cause, taking part in several of the most memorable battles of the war. He fought at the Battle of Bunker Hill in 1775, which the British won, though they suffered massive casualties, and also took part in the key American victory at the Battle of Saratoga. Shays worked his way up the military hierarchy, starting as a sergeant before being promoted to lieutenant. His record was impressive enough that not only did Shays earn the title of captain in the Continental Army in 1779, but the new rank was retroactively applied back to 1777.

———

Debt, both his own and the country's, turned Shays from a loyal fighter for the new nation to a revolutionary willing to fight against it.

The new country started out deeply in the red, because it had to borrow heavily from overseas and from wealthy Americans in order to help fund the revolution. Many of the soldiers returning from the war—including Daniel Shays—found themselves deep in personal debt. They hadn't earned very much during the revolution, and now they suddenly owed money they didn't have.

At this point, the United States also had no constitution, with the Articles of Confederation creating a weak central government with very limited powers—so limited it couldn't regulate things like trade or taxes—and giving the thirteen states most of the say. Each state had to pay its share of the war debt, and Massachusetts dealt with that burden by significantly raising taxes. On top of that, most of the people demanding their money back were demanding hard currency, which was a problem for Massachusetts farmers who were used to trading crops for needed goods rather than relying on metal money.

Some states had tried to address the related problems of farm and veteran debt by passing laws that eased the pressure on debtors, but Massachusetts didn't. Instead, the state foreclosed on farmers who owed taxes or other debts, and, since without a farm there was no possible income, broke men wound up in debtors' prisons.

Citizens sent one petition after another requesting help for debtors, but the state government continued its policy of taxation and harsh punishment for nonpayment. In August 1786, the state legislature met amid protests by Shays and other debtors, and still it refused to address their requests before the session ended.

Daniel Shays and Job Shattuck appear in this illustration from 1787.

While Shays didn't orchestrate this protest movement, he soon became its figurehead, leading thousands of protesters while dressed in his Revolutionary War uniform. Shays feared the mob could get out of control, and his status as both a fellow in-debt farmer and a war hero allowed him to serve as a credible leader for the angry debtors.

Shays and others figured that the courts could not foreclose on any more farms if the courts weren't in session. So, on August 29, Shays joined more than 1,000 armed protesters in marching on the courthouse in Northampton and successfully preventing the court from sitting. Soon, farmers were shutting down other courthouses. After the state supreme court indicted several leading rebels, Shays led an attempt to shut down that court, which was scheduled to reconvene on September 26. The state militia leader, General William Shepard, had put together a force to guard the courthouse, and was already in position when Shays and his men arrived. Instead of trying to take over the courthouse, Shays wound up merely leading a large demonstration on the grounds. That was still enough of a threat to get the court to delay opening and, two days later, to give up on the session and adjourn without hearing any cases.

On January 26, 1787, Shays led about 1,500 men to the federal armory in Springfield, planning to acquire better weapons and a barracks to use during the winter. When he got there, however, he found Shepard and his army already waiting for them. One of Shays's colleagues, who had about one third of the rebels under his command, had written Shays with the suggestion of pushing the attack back a day, but Shepard intercepted the message. After warning shots didn't turn back the rebels, Shepard's troops opened fire. Four of Shays's men were killed, another twenty were injured, and the rest fled throughout the area.

The governor of Massachusetts had already convened a militia of a few thousand state troops who, once word of the armory attack got around, pursued Shays's men. The rebellion was essentially over, as Shays and other ringleaders escaped to Vermont. Their supporters were either arrested, in hiding, or on the run.

While it was far from the only factor, and not his specific goal, Shays's Rebellion did help change the country's system of government. The rebellion, along with the federal debt crisis that prompted it, helped expose the dangers of a weak federal government. Less than four months after Shays's attempt on the armory, an already-planned convention to revise the Articles of Confederation met in Philadelphia. It emerged months later with the United States Constitution, and a stronger and more effective federal government.

MORE LIKE HIM

While Shays's Rebellion was probably the most influential, the United States had to contend with a number of uprisings by armed citizens in the early days of the country's independence. After Shays's, the two largest uprisings took place mainly in Pennsylvania, and both also started among farmers opposing taxation.

From 1791 to 1794, the Whiskey Rebellion involved Pennsylvania farmers (and a smaller number elsewhere in Appalachia) who protested new taxes on the leftover grain used to make whiskey—taxes that were being used to help pay off the war debt from the revolution. Tax opponents held conventions to plan resistance, but some took more extreme actions—such as attacking the home of a tax collector, covering another in tar and feathers, and burning another in effigy. In 1794, the situation escalated into violence before President George Washington sent a federal militia into the state and many of the rebel leaders fled.

Fries's Rebellion occurred a few years later, when John Fries led an armed group of Pennsylvania farmers to oppose a new real-estate tax. In 1799, Fries and his supporters harassed and even conducted "arrests" of tax assessors. Soon, the federal government began arresting people for tax evasion, and Fries and several supporters were arrested for treason when they tried to break some tax evaders out of jail.

In both cases, the leaders of the rebellions were pardoned by the president, a way of showing that the new government was more lenient than the one it had replaced, but would still put down any armed uprising against it.

As for Daniel Shays, he won in the end. The next state election brought in enough legislators sympathetic to debtors that many of the reforms Shays and his men had called for actually became law. Shays moved to New York from Vermont in 1788 after asking for and receiving a pardon (while hundreds were charged for their role in the rebellion, most received pardons or commuted sentences). He was seventy-eight when he died in Sparta, New York, in 1825. Ironically, Shays wound up drawing a federal pension as an old man, a reward for his actions during the Revolutionary War. ●

GEORGES DANTON

THE TIME: *1759–1794*

THE PLACE: *France*

THE OPPONENT: *The French monarchy*

J ust a few years after the American Revolution, the country that helped the colonies break free of Great Britain began its own revolution. Though the French Revolution began with similar ideas about liberty and equality, the new France that Georges Danton and others helped create was considerably less successful than the newly formed United States. Both it and Danton rose and fell in remarkably short order.

Under the leadership of its king, Louis XVI, France was in a bad spot when the revolution began. The king's support of the American colonies against Britain had cost a lot of money, and the new American nation was slow to pay its war debts. On top of that, the monarchy's spending had led to near-bankruptcy—it was not all Louis's fault, but he didn't help matters. French agriculture was in trouble after a series of prolonged droughts, livestock diseases, and poor harvests had made food prohibitively expensive. The poor and working classes had to pay high new taxes to make up for the country's debt, while unable to afford their basic needs. As the poor struggled, more than a few people noted that the rich and the royal weren't exactly going hungry.

By the spring of 1789, the situation had gotten so out of hand that the king had no choice but to summon the Estates General—a legislative body that hadn't held a meeting since 1614—and ask its members to come up with potential solutions to the country's various crises. Three estates made up the Estates General: the clergy, the nobility, and the people.

The common people made up more than 98 percent of the country, and their delegates (the Third Estate) wanted more say than those representing the other 2 percent. Since the first issue the Estates General had to consider was how to divide its power, that debate led to a predictable impasse. The Third Estate broke off and formed a new National Assembly, vowing to rule the country as that body.

———

Georges Danton had actually fared well under the existing governmental system. Born in 1759, he was a successful lawyer and married father by the time the revolution began, but he was nonetheless an early voice in favor of overthrowing the monarchy. Rather than being the brainchild of a sole revolutionary leader, the uprising in France came out of a series of political clubs, in which the people could meet and plan their rebellion. Danton became president of the Cordeliers, a club in Paris that prided itself on representing the common people; it played a large part in the start of the revolution.

Georges Jacques Danton in a not especially flattering engraving from the late eighteenth century.

Depending on who was describing him (he left few records of his own), Danton was either a true populist or a demagogue latching onto a popular idea as a way to obtain power. Either way, he became a vocal leader for the king's overthrow, using his great oratory to present his case. The Cordeliers were one of the clubs that took part in the storming of the Bastille, the July 14, 1789, attack on the royal prison in Paris (and the freeing of its seven prisoners). After Bastille Day, the people of Paris formed their own army, the National Guard, and its three-color flag became the symbol of the revolution (and remains the flag of France to this day).

Less than a month after the attack on the Bastille, the National Assembly passed the Declaration of the Rights of Man and of the Citizen, an official statement committing the legislature to governing based on democratic principles. The king was still technically in power; he just had little of it in reality.

———

Already an important man in Paris, Danton became even more of a leading national figure as power changed hands several times. In June 1791, the king and

A KINDER KILLING

Danton was hardly the only revolutionary in revolutionary France to literally lose his head in a revolutionary way. In 1789, a physician named Joseph-Ignace Guillotin proposed a new execution method, just in time for France to make full use of it.

Though Guillotin didn't invent the guillotine—and was actually opposed to the death penalty—the French version of the device was usually called by his name. Though the guillotine might seem gruesome by today's standards, he actually suggested it as a way to make execution more humane. Previous devices were designed to make torture and pain key components of an execution. Beheading happened quickly, and the power of the dropping blade made beheading by guillotine even faster and less painful. France continued to use it, right up until the country's final execution in 1977.

his wife tried and failed to flee the country. They were captured and brought back to Tuileries Palace, but the Assembly insisted it was still ruling a constitutional monarchy with Louis as king. On July 17, Danton led a crowd of protesters demanding the king's removal. The National Guard fired on them, killing about fifty. Danton briefly fled to London to avoid retaliation, but returned to Paris in time for the revolution's biggest victory.

On August 10, 1792, republican revolutionaries stormed Tuileries, exchanging fire with troops loyal to the king. The attack basically overthrew the constitutional monarchy, and (though his actual role in that day's uprising is disputed) Danton publicly took credit for the victory at Tuileries. His reputation, plus his political skill, got him elected minister of justice in the new government. The next year, France elected its National Convention—yet another attempt at a legislative body to run the country—and Danton was elected as the deputy from Paris.

Danton was among those who voted for the death penalty for the king, and on January 21, 1793, Louis XVI was publicly executed by guillotine on charges of high treason. On April 7, Danton was elected head of the Committee of Public Safety, yet another new body that ran the government, making Danton the most powerful man in France for three months. His rise to power, however, made him plenty of enemies. After the Jacobins—a more radical political faction, with whom Danton had allied earlier—took over the Committee in June, Danton tried to be a moderate voice. Some key Jacobins saw that as a betrayal.

As all the changes in government systems suggests, the leaders of the revolution were better at overthrowing power than at working together to hold it. Though the Committee approved France's first constitution that same June, it never went into effect. Instead, Maximilien de Robespierre, who replaced Danton as the most powerful man on the Committee, began a purge that became known as the Reign of Terror. Using as excuses both the ongoing war between France and other European powers and the legitimate arguments between Jacobins and moderates, he prosecuted tens of thousands as suspected enemies of the state—a definition that conveniently expanded to suit his needs.

The French Revolution famously devoured its own children, as in just ten months Robespierre and his allies brought "enemy of the revolution" charges against and executed somewhere between 15,000 and 50,000 French citizens (record keeping often slips during times of upheaval and chaos), most beheaded by guillotine.

Danton was no exception. Robespierre and other hard-liners viewed him with suspicion and searched for any excuse to charge him, eventually claiming it was for financial misdeeds. On April 5, 1794, one of the key architects of the revolution met his end, convicted without evidence or even witnesses, and executed by guillotine in Paris. "My only regret," Danton told the crowd, "is that I am going before that rat Robespierre." Robespierre didn't last much longer, executed on July 28 by his former Jacobin allies in a move that finally brought the Reign of Terror to an end.

With its violence and the purging of its leadership, French democracy was a failure at its start, a stark contrast to the sober experiment in elected government going on across the Atlantic. The National Convention continued for a few more years under more moderate leadership, but the democratic revolution ultimately failed. General Napoleon Bonaparte overthrew the government in a coup in November 1799, and declared himself emperor in 1804. It would be decades before France made another serious attempt at democratic rule. •

TECUMSEH

THE TIME: *1768–1813*

THE PLACE: *Shawnee territory*

THE OPPONENT: *United States*

In the early 1800s, many in the United States became obsessed with "manifest destiny," the idea of taking what started as a long strip of colonies and stretching it from sea to shining sea. Of course, that destiny would involve taking land from a lot of people already living there, who did their best to fight it. Few fought it as famously as the Shawnee war leader Tecumseh.

Tecumseh was born in 1768, near what's now Dayton, Ohio. Like a lot of revolutionary figures (including several in this book), he had reason to dislike his eventual adversary from an early age. When he was six, the colonial governor of Virginia sent a militia into Shawnee territory in Ohio, planning to enforce (at gunpoint) a territorial boundary—one that the British had agreed to in a treaty with the Iroquois nations, but one the Shawnee had rejected during negotiations and still didn't accept. A combined force of Shawnee and Mingo attacked the encroaching militia, fighting for hours in gruesome hand-to-hand combat, but the tribes lost badly and were forced to retreat. Tecumseh's father, Puckshinwa, was one of the Shawnee killed in the attack later named the Battle of Point Pleasant.

If losing his father wasn't enough, Tecumseh also lost his home repeatedly, as the family had to move three times when their villages were destroyed by American troops during and after the Revolutionary War. When several of the Native American nations in the Midwest formed an alliance in the 1780s to fight encroaching settlers, Tecumseh was eager to join. The alliance was usually outnumbered and outgunned in battle, but Tecumseh quickly made a name for himself with his tactical ability to lead raids and his rhetorical ability to inspire followers.

Both came in handy after the United States army, led by Revolutionary War veteran "Mad" Anthony Wayne, defeated the pan-Indian forces at the Battle of Fallen Timbers, in 1794. Most of the tribes signed a treaty that gave the federal government control over a large chunk of Ohio. Tecumseh refused to sign.

What Tecumseh understood, and made sure to explain to the Shawnee and others who continued to follow him, was that the United States was using a divide-and-conquer approach in dealing with native nations. It would form alliances with some tribes to fight others, and then turn on former allies once their mutual enemy was defeated. Tecumseh saw that the tribes that signed treaties and tried to adopt white ways were only putting off defeat, not escaping it. As he later put it in a speech to the Chickasaw and Choctaw, "The annihilation of our race is at hand unless we unite in one common cause against one common foe."

One way Tecumseh united his supporters was to team up with his younger brother, Tenskwatawa, whose mystic visions and religious preaching earned him the nickname "the Prophet." Tenskwatawa advocated complete separation between the tribes and white Americans, and thus a complete rejection of any food, customs, or lifestyle that came from the newcomers. The Prophet's religious movement gained supporters when he made a few big predictions that

Tecumseh in action during the War of 1812 (from a c. 1860 print).

came true—for example, the day of a solar eclipse—and his prediction of an ultimate victory against the white man seemed more plausible.

In 1808, the two brothers founded their own settlement of Tippecanoe in northwest Indiana (often called "Prophetstown" by both friends and enemies), where their combined charisma drew followers from numerous tribes. Many came for the religious teachings of his brother, but Tecumseh also began to form them into a unified, pan-Indian settlement that soon became the largest Native American settlement in the Great Lakes and the best chance at a successful stand against the American settlers who kept pushing west.

The settlement wasn't a secret to American officials, who were disturbed to see the Great Lakes tribes come together under a powerful leader. William Henry Harrison, the governor of the Indiana territory, had started buying up land from some of the regional tribes, including more than three million acres in the 1810 Treaty of Ft. Wayne—land that included Tippecanoe. Tecumseh even met with Harrison, arguing that the treaty was illegitimate and his settlement wanted only peace and to be left alone, but their meeting ended without much accomplished except for mutual threats. The Prophet continued to amp up the tension, making numerous death threats against Harrison. Knowing battle couldn't be far off, Tecumseh set off to recruit more tribes to join his growing confederacy.

With Tecumseh off on his mission, Harrison saw an opportunity. On November 6, 1811, he showed up at Prophetstown with an army of about 1,000 men and agreed to meet with Tenskwatawa the next day for a negotiation. Who deserves the blame for what happened next is still unclear, and depends on

CURSES

To those who believe in such things, Tecumseh got his revenge on Harrison with a curse delivered by his brother. Harrison was elected president of the United States in 1840, but he managed two dubious achievements—serving just thirty-two days (the shortest tenure ever) before dying of pneumonia and becoming the first American president to die in office.

Harrison also started a pattern, since for a time every president elected in a year ending in zero died in office, allegedly (but not really) because of the curse. Abraham Lincoln, James Garfield, William McKinley, Warren Harding, Franklin Roosevelt, and John Kennedy continued the pattern for more than a century, regularly reviving the legend of the "Curse of Tecumseh" (also called the "Curse of Tippecanoe"). The streak ended with Ronald Reagan, elected in 1980, and he survived being shot early in his presidency.

whether Harrison or Tenskwatawa, or both, was telling the truth about wanting a peaceful outcome. What is clear, however, is that a group of warriors from Tippecanoe attacked Harrison's camp overnight, and the Americans responded by driving off the Prophet's forces and burning down Prophetstown.

Tippecanoe put Tecumseh in a terrible position, taking away his ability to win a war while also making peace impossible. His brother's credibility among the tribes disappeared, since he'd predicted a great victory, and now Tecumseh had a lot of work to do just to rebuild an alliance. He found a valuable ally in Great Britain, and teamed up with the king's forces in Canada for important battles against the United States in the War of 1812. Tecumseh's masterstroke in the war came when he helped the British take Detroit, using a strategic marching formation to make it look like he had a lot more troops than he really did, and scaring the city into surrender.

The success, however, didn't last long. American forces captured Detroit the next year, and the combined British and Native American forces retreated into Canada, where they were soon pursued by Tecumseh's old nemesis, Harrison. A fighter until the end, Tecumseh was killed by Harrison's forces on October 15, 1813, at the Battle of the Thames. Who exactly killed him remains uncertain, and his body wasn't recovered. But his death prompted most of his confederacy to surrender, ending Native American resistance in the region.

Even Tecumseh's enemies acknowledged him as a worthy adversary. Richard Johnson became famous by claiming to be the one who killed Tecumseh in battle, and he eventually used that fame to become vice president under Martin Van Buren in 1836. The victory at Tippecanoe was seen as big enough that Harrison used it as the basis for his successful presidential campaign in 1840. William Tecumseh Sherman, the brutally effective Union general who brought destruction to the South during the Civil War, was named after him. Today, schools and towns throughout the United States and Canada bear his name, many of them ironically located in areas that the Shawnee and their compatriots were forced to leave. ●

SHAKING ALL OVER

Harrison wasn't the only supposed victim of a Tecumseh-related prediction. In December 1811, the two biggest earthquakes ever recorded in the eastern United States hit just a few hours apart. Though both were centered on the New Madrid fault line in northeastern Arkansas, there were reports of shaking as far away as Boston and Washington, D.C.

Shortly before the quake, Tecumseh had told a Creek ally that when he arrived in Detroit, he would stomp his foot and the ground would shake. His tough-guy talk seemed like a prophecy when the New Madrid quakes hit on the same day he got to Detroit.

Bolívar swaggers silently in this 1819 engraving by M. N. Bate.

SIMÓN BOLÍVAR

THE TIME: *1783–1830*

THE PLACE: *South America*

THE OPPONENT: *Spain*

Simón Bolívar's revolutions proved the adage that it can be a lot easier to overthrow a government than to replace it. However, even in his lifetime the man called "El Libertador" created quite a legacy, turning six current countries from Spanish colonies into parts of independent nations. Modern South America wouldn't look nearly the same without him.

When Bolívar was born in 1783, most of South America (with Brazil being the most notable exception) was still ruled by Spain. While he was born in Caracas, Venezuela, Bolívar's family line descended from wealthy Spanish aristocrats. Though he was orphaned at age nine, Bolívar's inheritance gave him the means for a top education, including three years of study in Spain. He married a woman he met there and they returned to Venezuela, but, after she died from yellow fever within a year, he moved to France in 1804.

Bolívar's time in France in his early twenties inspired what would become his life's pursuit—bringing liberty to South America. He devoured books by Enlightenment thinkers like John Locke and Thomas Hobbes, and taught himself about the recent revolutions in America and France. His vision became to form a South American republic out of a coalition of states, similar to the system the young United States had developed.

He returned to Caracas in 1807, and Bolívar got his chance to enact his ideals quickly, as revolutionary rumblings were already growing. In 1809, Napoleon Bonaparte of France surprised Spain by suddenly breaking the countries' alliance

THE NAME LIVES ON

The country of Bolivia still bears the name of Simón Bolívar, but it's hardly alone. Venezuela's full name remains the Bolivarian Republic of Venezuela. Colombia named one of its states after him, and one of the country's tallest mountains is Pico Simón Bolívar. Nine South American countries are parties to the ALBA (Alianza Bolivariana para los Pueblos de Nuestra América) trade treaty, known in English as the Bolivarian Alliance for the Peoples of Our America. Monuments to Bolívar have been erected not only throughout South America, but in numerous other countries, including the United States, Egypt, Turkey, and France.

and invading, forcing the Spanish government to take its eye off its South American colonies for a bit. Bolívar joined a Caracas-based junta movement that was plotting a rebellion and on April 19, 1810, the junta managed to kick out Spain's regional governor and declare itself the new government.

Of course, that was just the first step. Bolívar and other members of the junta traveled to Great Britain in the hopes of getting the British to recognize an independent Venezuela. After all, Great Britain was where Francisco de Miranda—a Venezuelan who had tried unsuccessfully to start his own revolution in 1806—had gone into exile. Though that didn't work, while in Great Britain the Venezuelan contingent also met with Miranda and convinced him to return and lead the new country.

The arrangement worked nicely at first. Miranda had the revolutionary credibility to convince the acting government to make a formal break from Spain. In March 1811, a convention was held to pass a new constitution, and on July 5 the country finally declared independence.

The First Republic of Venezuela had been created . . . and it lasted barely a year. Pro-royal forces advanced from both directions, and their victories included capturing the port city where Bolívar was in charge, after one or more of his men betrayed the cause. His army losing badly, Miranda negotiated an armistice and ceded control back to Spain in July 1812. Bolívar and some others saw that as a betrayal, and retaliated by turning him over to the enemy (Miranda would die in prison). As for Simón Bolívar, he left the country to plan his next move.

Bolívar made a second attempt at establishing an independent Venezuela in 1813. This time, he was leading an invasion from Cartagena, Colombia (then part of a larger, short-lived nation called New Granada). There, he had published *El Manifiesto de Cartagena*, in which he laid out his vision for South America, blaming the fall of the last Venezuelan republic on a weak central government.

His work earned enough support that the army of New Granada gave him troops and supplies to try to free its neighbor to the east again.

Bolívar fought six battles against pro-Spain forces in what was called his "Admirable Campaign," lasting between January and August of 1813, and he pushed his way to Caracas and recaptured the city. On this campaign, he took the stance that any Spaniard who didn't actively help the revolutionary cause should be killed, though he spared native Venezuelans. He also named himself dictator once the fighting seemed to conclude, and declared a Second Venezuelan Republic.

Despite his new tactics, the outcome this time wasn't that different. Bolívar ruled for about a year before Spanish-backed forces mounted a counteroffensive, retook Caracas and other major cities, crushed the republic, and forced Bolívar to flee the country in 1814.

Simón Bolívar could have been forgiven for giving up after twice seeing his republican dream fall apart. Instead, he dreamed bigger.

By 1815, he was living in Jamaica, and a letter he penned while there has proven his most enduring political writing. In his *Carta de Jamaica* (*Letter from Jamaica*) he reflected on his previous pursuits of liberation and what went wrong before. The big takeaway was the importance of the push for the countries of South America to not only win independence, but become allies against any colonial powers.

The next round of freedom fighting was what really made Simón Bolívar's legend.

Though his 1816 revolution once again began in Venezuela, he switched his target to liberating New Granada, which Spain had reconquered while he was abroad. With only about 2,500 men, including a legion the British had sent to assist him, he crossed the Andes Mountains from his base in southwestern Venezuela—a move Spanish forces didn't see coming.

Bolívar won a few smaller battles before a huge win at the Battle of Boyacá on August 7, 1819, in which he captured 1,800 Spanish fighters and their commander. Three days later, he took the capital city of Bogotá and declared a provisional government in what he named the republic of Gran Colombia. In December, he organized a congress for the new republic, which named him president and commander of the military.

Much of what he considered part of Gran Colombia was still technically Spanish territory, and Bolívar set about undoing that. In June 1821, he retook Caracas and liberated Venezuela (for good this time). In May 1822, he captured Quito and crossed Ecuador off his checklist.

Also in 1822, he took over the war against Spain in Peru from Jose de San Martin, the revolutionary from Argentina who had been waging his

PARALLEL LINES

Just as the American Revolution probably couldn't have succeeded if Great Britain wasn't also fighting a war with France, the French invasion of Spain was a huge help to Bolívar's early attempts at revolution. By 1809, Napoleon controlled most of Spain, which fought back in its own successful War of Independence. For his part, Napoleon called the experience his "Spanish ulcer," and blamed his defeats in other parts of Europe on the Spanish War taking up resources he needed elsewhere.

own rebellion from the south. It took some time to defeat the Spanish forces in the mountains around the capital of Lima, but in February 1824, Bolívar was named dictator of Peru. The following year, the territory of Upper Peru (to the east of Peru itself)—the last stronghold of pro-Spanish royalists—fell to Antonio José de Sucre, Bolívar's number-two man. Upper Peru changed its name to Bolivia, and its legislature elected Bolívar its president.

In just a decade, Simón Bolívar and his supporters had overthrown Spanish rule in what are now Venezuela, Colombia, Panama, Ecuador, Peru, and Bolivia. Though he was in command of the entire operation, so much land and so many factions proved unwieldy to control. Uprisings were already starting in Venezuela by 1826, and actual war broke out between commanders in Venezuela and the old New Granada. An 1828 convention to create a new constitution for Gran Colombia collapsed, with factions unable to come to any agreement.

Some of those factions had also started to consider Bolívar himself and his dictatorial power—power he did agree to give up on a specific future date—part of the problem. On September 25, 1828, he was attacked by would-be assassins who tried to stab him in his own palace, but he escaped without injury. No less painful for him was the news that his homeland of Venezuela seceded from the rest of Gran Colombia in the fall of 1829, ending any hope of the South American cooperative he'd devoted his life to creating. "Independence is the only benefit we have gained," Bolívar said during this period, "at the cost of everything else."

Seeing his creation falling apart and feeling his presence was doing more harm than good, Bolívar resigned his office on April 27, 1830, and planned to go into self-imposed exile in Europe. Before leaving, he received word that his handpicked successor, Antonio José de Sucre, had been assassinated, and delayed his trip. Only forty-seven at the time, he died of tuberculosis during that delay, on December 17, 1830. ●

NAT TURNER

THE TIME: *1800–1831*

THE PLACE: *United States*

THE OPPONENT: *Slavery*

Though a relatively small-scale revolt, the attack carried out by Nat Turner and his recruits sent terror through the slaveholding states of the American South. The fighting lasted only one night, but its legacy endured far longer.

Nathaniel "Nat" Turner was born in 1800, the child of slaves on a plantation in Southampton County, Virginia. The surname Turner came from Benjamin Turner, the master who owned the boy's mother and grandmothers (his father is believed to have escaped when Nat was young). Though a field slave, Turner learned to read and write as a young boy, and also became deeply religious at an early age.

Supposedly, Turner displayed strange tendencies as a child, describing events from before his birth and adopting ascetic religious practices, like fasting and praying alone rather than socializing. At some point, he earned a reputation as a prophet among his fellow slaves, and sometimes led religious services for them.

While he had a desire to live free from slavery, which obviously played a role in his 1831 uprising, Turner also had religious reasons for his actions. He claimed to have divine visions, and based decisions on those visions well before the rebellion. When he was twenty-two, he managed to escape and live free for about a month, but he came back to the Turner estate based on a vision in which a spirit told him to return to his "earthly master."

Like many slaves, Nat Turner changed hands repeatedly; he was sold three different times before he had to work for John Travis, the man he would later kill. In 1822, he was sold to Thomas Moore, another Southampton County plantation owner. Turner claimed he had another prophetic vision there, one filled with imagery like corn covered in blood in the fields he worked.

PART OF A PATTERN

One reason Nat Turner's revolt got so much attention was that it fit a pattern of planned slave revolts around the same time. He simply managed to pull it off more successfully—and with a serious body count.

The same month that Nat Turner was born in 1800, a slave named Gabriel had planned a rebellion in Richmond, Virginia, but was discovered and hanged before he could carry it out. A similar situation took place in South Carolina in 1822, when freed slave Denmark Vesey was caught plotting an attack. In the territory that later became Louisiana, an 1811 slave revolt only killed two white men, but it did feature the largest number of slaves rebelling together in American history.

Another vision arrived a few years later, in which Turner said Jesus put down a yoke representing the burden of mankind's sins and told him to pick it up and "fight the serpent." As Turner put it later, the vision told him, "I should arise and prepare myself and slay my enemies with their own weapons."

By the time that preparation began in earnest, Turner was technically owned by a child named Putnam Moore, who was the son of Turner's previous owner. Thomas Moore's widow, however, had married John Travis, who made Turner and other slaves work his land. Turner saw a cosmic endorsement of his revolt in February 1831, taking a solar eclipse as a sign from God urging him to move ahead with his plan.

Turner originally planned for the uprising to take place on July 4, as a bloody reminder on Independence Day that many in America still lacked independence. For various reasons, he had to delay his plan, until another eclipse on August 13 (one that reportedly made the sun look an unusual blue-green color) convinced Turner he shouldn't wait any longer to start killing the people who kept him in slavery.

Other slave revolts of the early 1800s had failed before they started, due to slave owners learning of the plot or less-rebellious slaves tipping them off. Turner wisely kept his inner circle small, trusting only a handful of slaves he knew well. His rebellion would eventually include more than seventy slaves, but most had too little advance information to put the uprising at risk.

On August 21, 1831, Turner and his small team carried out their plans. In order to maintain an element of surprise, Turner had his men leave their guns behind and instead use handheld weapons—such as knives, axes, and hatchets—to kill almost every white person they encountered that night.

They started with the Travis household, killing the master and his entire family in their sleep. From there, the men moved from one house to another, killing the owners and recruiting more slaves to their cause. They obtained horses and weapons along the way, and left few survivors in the households they attacked (in one famous example, a young girl survived by hiding in a fireplace until Turner's men left). However, despite the stated goal of killing as many whites as possible, Turner said they intentionally passed certain homes belonging to poor whites, choosing to focus on those who held power and slaves.

Benjamin Phipps captures Nat Turner in this engraving from 1831.

On the afternoon of August 22, Turner and his men headed toward Jerusalem, the city nearest to the plantations they'd attacked. At that point, word of what Turner was up to had gotten around, and a militia arrived to stop him. Because most of his men were recruits who had joined just that day, Turner had trouble keeping his forces together, and two waves of attacks—first from the militia, then from state and federal troops—managed to end the rebellion and result in the arrest of most of the rebels, though Turner escaped capture.

He and his men killed at least fifty-five people in the attacks. By his account, Turner had no illusions that his revolt would end slavery or that he would outlive the mission. His goal was to "spread terror and alarm" among slave owners, making them understand slavery was a violent system, and that the violence could work in both directions.

Ironically, considering the amount of manpower the state was using to find him, Turner was discovered on October 30 by a farmer named Benjamin Phipps, who was simply out hunting when he came across a hole where the revolutionary leader was hiding. Turner pled not guilty at trial, arguing that he was doing divine work, and admitted to killing only one of the victims himself.

A PUBLISHING SENSATION

Word of Turner's rebellion reached far beyond Virginia, thanks to a best-selling pamphlet. Much of what the public knew about Turner at the time came from that account.

A local lawyer (though not, as often reported, Turner's lawyer), Thomas Ruffin Gray, published *The Confessions of Nat Turner* with the stated goal of creating a definitive, true version of an event that was already spawning wild stories.

Gray visited and interviewed Turner in jail on November 1, wrote down his "full, free and voluntary" confession, and copyrighted the material nine days later. The confession was used as evidence against Turner during the trial, and certainly sensationalized parts of the story. However, Gray's preface to the book showed a certain respect for Turner by portraying him as honest and intelligent—as someone who was taking full responsibility for his actions.

The story found a new audience in 1967, during the heyday of the civil rights movement, when author William Styron (later well-known for *Sophie's Choice*) crafted a highly fictionalized version of Turner's life, using the same title as Gray's book. Though controversial for some of the liberties it took, the book won the Pulitzer Prize for fiction and appeared on various critics' lists of the best American novels.

Sentenced to death, Turner was hanged in Jerusalem, Virginia, on November 11. Not content with just killing him, the authorities mutilated his corpse—flaying it, beheading it, and quartering what was left. Virginia executed fifty-six other slaves charged with taking part in Turner's plot, and that wasn't the worst of it. As early as August, pro-slavery whites responded to Turner's actions with a series of vigilante attacks against random African-Americans, most of whom had nothing to do with Turner or his rebellion. More than 200 people died in the mob violence, and an unknown number were injured.

Nat Turner's rebellion immediately became a message to abolitionists that violence was inevitable if slavery continued. He became a hero to many in the years leading up to the Civil War, and his rebellion also served as an important reminder to the South and supporters of slavery that there were many more slaves than slave owners, and that the same thing could happen on their plantations. ●

JOHN BROWN

THE TIME: *1800–1859*

THE PLACE: *United States*

THE OPPONENT: *Slavery*

John Brown wasn't the first to take up arms in the fight to end slavery in the United States, and he was far from the most successful. Nonetheless, the abolitionist's bold actions—and his insistence that the crusade against slavery demanded violence, since talk had failed—played an important part in escalating the conflict between states and bringing about the civil war that ended slavery for good.

Born in Connecticut in 1800, John Brown grew up in a household that opposed slavery, with a father committed to doing what he could to fight it. Brown had a full but often complicated life. He was father to twenty children with two women (his first wife died in 1832, and a few of the children died very young). He moved many times, living in Ohio, Massachusetts, Pennsylvania, and New York, and tried his hand at a number of careers with varying degrees of success.

For all that change, his belief in the abolition of slavery remained constant. After a terrible run of bad luck in Ohio—in about a year's time, he went bankrupt and four of his children died—Brown moved with his business partner to Springfield, Massachusetts, in 1846. There, he began turning his beliefs into action. He adopted a black child, met slave-turned-abolitionist Frederick Douglass, and helped with the activities of the Underground Railroad. He even briefly moved to North Elba, New York, to live among escaped slaves and donate land to them. When Congress passed the 1850 Fugitive Slave Act—a law that cracked down on slaves who escaped to the North and rewarded those who returned them—Brown responded by starting a group called the League of Gileadites. The armed militia promised to protect any escaped slaves in Springfield from getting recaptured (and none were, after that point).

His track record of opposing slavery and his religious fury for the cause meant it was only a matter of time before John Brown wound up in Kansas.

The United States had barely avoided war over slavery with the Missouri Compromise of 1820. Prior to that, the country had exactly as many free states as slave states, but Missouri applying for statehood risked swinging that balance. The growing opposition to slavery saw a chance to help stop its spread, and Southern states that had built their economic system on slavery fought hard to keep it. The Speaker of the House of Representatives, Henry Clay, spearheaded an agreement that brought Missouri into the Union as a slave state but also brought in Maine as a free state, keeping the balance, and kicking the slavery issue down the road for the next generation to solve.

That tension came up again when Congress created territories out of Kansas and Nebraska. Under the 1854 Kansas-Nebraska Act, the pro- or anti-slavery status of the two future states would be decided by "popular sovereignty," meaning the votes of their people. Nebraska was sufficiently northern to be an automatic free state, but Kansas's fate was far less clear. Considering how much tension already existed between the supporters and opponents of slavery, the act predictably led to violent battles. Both factions tried to fix the outcome, flooding the state with supporters, and setting up rival territorial governments. The state earned the nickname "Bleeding Kansas" as the fighting between the two sides turned violent (though many were injured, the death toll was fairly small).

At age fifty-five, Brown moved into the thick of the Kansas chaos, with five of his adult sons. He set up a militia of anti-slavery men, and after slavery supporters attacked the city of Lawrence in May 1856, Brown chose to take revenge. On May 24, John Brown and a few others attacked a pro-slavery settle-

John Brown is staring, c. 1850.

ment near Pottawatomie Creek, ordering five unarmed men out of their homes at night and killing them with swords.

The Pottawatomie Massacre set off the worst strife yet in Kansas, but Brown left for the Northeast, trying to raise funds for his next plan—an armed uprising in Virginia, the heart of the South. His plan involved creating a base in the northern part of the state, where slaves could both escape and join the rebellion. He rented a farm for that purpose, and started building a guerilla army.

Brown's conviction that only violence could end slavery (and his murders of unarmed men in Kansas) made some in abolitionist circles deem him a terrorist hurting the cause, but he did gain enough support (including financial support) to think his plan could work.

On October 16, 1859, John Brown made his name in history by leading a racially mixed force of twenty-one men into Harper's Ferry, Virginia, and seizing control of the federal armory.

Taking the arsenal proved easier than holding it. Though the raid went well at first, Brown's men weren't able to take the weapons and skip town before a B&O Railroad crew alerted the federal government about the raid. The marines were on the scene by the afternoon of October 17, led by future Confederate general Robert E. Lee. Brown's men, who had already fought townspeople and taken hostages, were holed up in an engine house when Lee's men stormed

FROM HARPER'S TO HARPERS

Harper's Ferry, Virginia, the site of John Brown's famous raid, is now Harpers Ferry, West Virginia (minus the apostrophe). Because of its location at the meeting of the Shenandoah and Potomac Rivers, the town was captured and recaptured eight times during the Civil War, during which West Virginia split off from Virginia and became a Union state. Part of Harpers Ferry became a national monument in 1944. It soon became a national historical park and remains so today, drawing about half a million visitors per year.

it the next day. It took just three minutes for the marines to arrest Brown and his remaining associates. (Ten of his men, including two of his sons, had died during the raid on Harper's Ferry.)

Though the armory he attacked was on federal land, Brown was tried in Virginia under state law—probably the state's attempt to avoid leniency. On November 2, the jury found Brown guilty on all three counts, and his execution was scheduled for the next month.

Brown had his defenders at the time—writers like Victor Hugo, Henry David Thoreau, and Ralph Waldo Emerson expressed support, with Emerson comparing the upcoming execution to that of Jesus on the cross. The raid and the trial made Brown famous, and his correspondence from prison showed he also considered himself a martyr to the cause of ending slavery.

On December 2, John Brown was hanged for his raid on Harper's Ferry. His body was buried in North Elba, where he had lived among former slaves. On the morning of his execution, he famously wrote that he was "now quite certain that the crimes of this guilty land will never be purged away but with blood." Just thirteen months later, Abraham Lincoln became president, the South seceded, and the country truly began the violent reckoning with slavery that Brown had tried to start. •

GIUSEPPE GARIBALDI

THE TIME: *1807–1882*

THE PLACES: *Italy, Uruguay*

THE OPPONENTS: *Austria, France, Argentina*

Few revolutionaries can take credit for the independence of more than one country, much less countries with as little in common as Italy and Uruguay. The Italian military commander Giuseppe Garibaldi could make that claim.

Garibaldi was born on July 4, 1807, in the Italian city of Nice, when that part of Italy was under the control of France and part of Napoleon Bonaparte's European empire. Garibaldi's early career focused on sailing, as he joined the family business and became a captain by the time he was twenty-five. He took a position in the navy of Piedmont-Sardinia, one of the many then-separate Italian states.

In 1833, he met Giuseppe Mazzini, an exiled activist already committed to Italian unification, who was plotting a rebellion to bring about an Italian republic. The following year, Garibaldi led one part of Mazzini's planned uprisings in Piedmont, albeit an unsuccessful one. When the mutiny failed, Garibaldi skipped town, heading to France for a short time before sailing to North Africa and then to South America in 1836. A court sentenced him to death in absentia, and Garibaldi couldn't return to his homeland without risking arrest and execution. Though he spent more than a decade in exile, Garibaldi put that time to good use, establishing his revolutionary bona fides abroad.

He got his first real military experience in Brazil, where in 1839 he joined up with the "Ragamuffins," a rebel force based in Rio Grande do Sul. That southernmost state was trying to become a republic independent from the rest of the Brazilian Empire, and to establish another republic to its north in Santa Catarina. Garibaldi mostly aided the Ragamuffins by fighting Brazilian ships near the coast. When the rebellion failed and Rio Grande eventually conceded defeat,

UNITED, BUT WITH DIVISIONS

Though Italy has remained a country for more than 150 years, it still shows the signs of the patchwork of city-states it used to be. As Italian statesman Massimo d'Azeglio said at the time of unification, "We have made Italy. Now we have to make Italians." It's not uncommon for Italians to identify as Tuscans or Neapolitans first, and some regions still have distinct, historical differences in what languages are spoken there. Plus, two of the world's smallest countries—San Marino and the Vatican City—exist completely within the borders of Italy.

Garibaldi and his new girlfriend—whom he had met during the rebellion and who served aboard his ship, the *Rio Pravo*—drove cattle to Uruguay. There, they married (overlooking the fact that she was already married to someone else), and Garibaldi took a teaching job while embracing the gaucho (cowboy) lifestyle. It didn't take him long, however, to take up another revolutionary cause.

———————

Garibaldi had better luck with revolution in Uruguay, where he served as head of the Uruguayan navy in its fight against Argentina. By 1843, he had also organized a full legion of Italian ground troops under his command (mostly exiles like himself). The uniform that Garibaldi wore for the rest of his life came from his time leading this group of "Redshirts," so named because of the red wool shirts they wore. His men won an impressive victory at San Antonio del Santo, and in 1847 helped defend the capital Montevideo against a siege by Argentine forces.

Both the siege and the San Antonio victory became international news, earning Garibaldi and his guerilla tactics fame back in Italy. By 1848, a number of Italian states had started to rebel against their occupying powers, with many supporting Garibaldi's old comrade Mazzini's goal of a united Italian republic.

Garibaldi remained a firm supporter of Risorgimento, the movement to unify the Italian states, so he left Uruguay in the middle of its war and returned to Italy with about sixty members of his Redshirts. Garibaldi was a charismatic leader, the type who could energize his men with a rousing speech and make Mazzini's goal of an Italian republic something that seemed worth risking their lives for.

His first challenge was finding an Italian leader whom he could champion. The new pope, Pius IX, turned down Garibaldi's offer to fight for him. So did the king of Piedmont-Sardinia, who knew Garibaldi had been exiled and that he supported a republic (which even the most pro-unification king didn't exactly want). The third attempt was the charm, as Milan took his offer of help.

Milan was part of the northern Italian Kingdom of Lombardy-Venetia, then ruled by the Austrian Empire. Garibaldi's Redshirts defeated the Austrian forces in battle at Lunio and again at Morazzone, while other rebels succeeded at driving some Austrian troops out of Milan. These all proved minor victories, however, and the First Italian War for Independence lasted little more than a year.

Garibaldi fled to Switzerland after his failure in Milan, but was back in Italy later in 1849, leading volunteers to Rome in April. The Rome-based Papal States had driven out the pope and declared their own republic, and France sent an army to overthrow the republic. The Redshirts won an early victory (and achieved worldwide fame for their bravery) by fighting back the French invaders, but France sent reinforcements and placed Rome under siege.

The Papal States agreed to surrender in July, despite Garibaldi urging them to fight on, and he was forced to retreat with about four thousand troops. The would-be unifier of Italy had to abandon that land again, taking an extended trip that lasted nearly five years, with stops in San Marino, Morocco, the United States, Peru, and the United Kingdom.

Though his military campaigns had produced very mixed results, Garibaldi was still considered to be a legendary leader who inspired patriotism among Italians. The prime minister of Piedmont, Camillo Benso, recognized this, and allowed Garibaldi to come back in the hope of getting him to fight for a unified Italy without pushing for a republic.

Garibaldi returned to Italy in 1854 to begin farming on an island he purchased near Sardinia. As Piedmont was preparing for the Second Italian War of Independence, Camillo Benso made a secret deal with France for support against Austria, and commissioned Garibaldi to lead a volunteer unit in the north. This group, nicknamed the "Hunters of the North," captured Varese and Como from the Austrians, and the war ended with a Piedmont victory.

As part of the secret terms of the alliance with France, Piedmont ceded the areas of Savoy and Nice to the French. Seeing his home region go back under

Garibaldi seems pretty confident in this photo from 1866.

A KING IN NAME

Just because Italy had a king from 1861 until 1946 didn't mean the monarchy truly ruled the country that entire time. Most famously, the fascist dictator Benito Mussolini was clearly in charge from 1925 until 1943, though he technically came to power as prime minister and then used that office to make his dictatorship legal. On the other hand, it was King Victor Emanuel III who finally removed him from office and had him arrested (a bit late). Mussolini escaped and spent his last years ruling a German client state in northern Italy before his arrest and execution by Communist partisans.

French control for the first time since his boyhood felt like a betrayal to Garibaldi. Still, he fought on.

In 1860, he led an army of volunteers onto the island of Sicily in support of republican uprisings in Palermo and Messina. At the Battle of Calatafimi on May 15, he led an uphill charge that defeated a fortification housing an army nearly twice the size of his. He named himself dictator of Sicily in the name of the king (while he'd soured on the prime minister, he still saw the king as the best route to creating one unified Italy). With help from the British, Garibaldi marched on and took Palermo, then sailed to Naples and captured that city on September 7. His strategy of quick strikes and guerrilla tactics had worked, as his army kept the pressure on the enemy and he captured a huge swath of Italy in just a few months.

In March 1861, the liberated territories were declared a united kingdom of Italy, with Victor Emanuel II crowned its first king. Though Garibaldi always supported the unification, he was consistently critical of the new kingdom. Despite his reservations, Garibaldi continued to carry out military campaigns for Italy—against French control of the Papal States, against Austria in the Austro-Prussian War, and in a successful conquest of Venice that returned it to Italy. He was arrested by the Italian government in 1867 after he was wounded during an illegal (but quietly supported) attack against the French in the Papal States, though he was released soon afterward. His last campaign came in 1870, when he helped Italy's former occupier, France, in its war with Prussia, and made enough of an impression to get elected to the French legislature.

Garibaldi had wanted simply to unify Italy, not to lead it, and that humility helped make him a national hero. He eventually retired to a government pension, though he continued to speak out about current affairs (such as racial equality and labor rights, both of which he supported) until his death at seventy-four on June 2, 1882. ●

HONE HEKE

THE TIME: *c. 1807–1850*

THE PLACE: *New Zealand*

THE OPPONENT: *British settlers*

Compared to its conquests of most of its territories, Britain's addition of New Zealand to the British sphere of influence was relatively peaceful—at least at first. Still, some Maori leaders, Hone Heke among them, bristled under the dramatic changes brought by British rule, and their protests turned into rebellion.

Hone Wiremu Heke Pokai was born around 1807, near the Bay of Islands in the far northwestern part of New Zealand. Like many native New Zealanders, he was educated in a missionary school, and grew up a Christian, but he first gained his reputation by fighting in a series of battles between Maori tribes.

The Maori originated elsewhere in Polynesia and settled New Zealand (called Aotearoa in Maori) by the thirteenth century (if not earlier), traveling great distances by sea. Though they shared a common language and heritage, the tribes also had a long history of fighting one another over territory (and, in the early days, of eating the defeated).

The same year Hone Heke was born, several Maori *iwi* (groupings similar to tribes) began a series of conflicts known

Hone Heke and his wife, Hariata, becloaked in flax, in fact.

as the Musket Wars, which lasted decades and included thousands of battles. Hone Heke's iwi, the Ngapuhi, was among the first to acquire guns.

His uncle Hongi Hika, then the war leader of the iwi, traveled to Australia and negotiated with visiting traders to acquire more weapons, which he and his war parties used to dominate the North Island and kill thousands of rival iwi members. When he came of age, Hone Heke joined the Musket Wars, distinguishing himself in combat in the north.

Hongi Hika also traded land for weapons, encouraging Europeans to settle in the north of New Zealand. These settlements brought more commerce, new technologies, and religious missions to the islands. However, because New Zealand had a large territory and relatively few people, it also became a popular spot for troublemakers to settle, with escaped convicts, disreputable sailors, and other undesirables coming ashore and committing crimes. At the same time, France was actively expanding its territory in the South Pacific, and the Maori wanted nothing to do with French occupation.

In 1831, a group of thirteen Maori chiefs wrote a letter to the king of England, William IV, petitioning for Aotearoa to come under his protection. The king agreed, and in 1833 sent a resident to help transition the territory into British rule. A few years later, he sent William Hobson—who would become the first British governor of what would become New Zealand—to negotiate a handover with the Maori chiefs.

On February 6, 1840, Hone Heke was the first of forty-five northern Maori chiefs to sign the Treaty of Waitangi, the formal agreement giving sovereignty to the crown. The treaty gave the Maori rights of British citizenship, and essentially created the nation of New Zealand as a concept.

What "sovereignty" meant, of course, came across differently in the translated version of the treaty. By 1842, Hone Heke had become convinced that the new arrangement, rather than creating the shared-power situation he and the other chiefs had expected, made British authorities too dominant.

Part of the problem was economic. The British had relocated the capital of New Zealand from Kororareka to Auckland, moving the heart of the economy with it. A British association called the New Zealand Company had started organizing large-scale British immigration to the territory, establishing new cities like Wellington and Nelson. British trade laws called for adding customs to imports, making goods more expensive, and giving all tax revenue to the crown. Beyond the economic problems caused by the new treaty, there was also a shift in power. One controversy that particularly angered Hone Heke involved the son of a northern chief who murdered a white family and was hanged in 1842— by a crown-backed authority, without Maori input.

RIGHTING WRONGS

In 1975, the government of New Zealand set up the Waitangi Tribunal, a legal mechanism to consider complaints about treaty violations. At first, it only allowed Maori to bring claims dating from after the tribunal's creation, but it soon expanded to consider any grievances Maori had about possible violations of the Treaty of Waitangi's terms. Though it isn't a court (it makes recommendations to the government, not binding decisions), the tribunal has helped settle grievances through payment for confiscated land, recognition of iwi rights, or formal apologies from the government (including one delivered personally by Queen Elizabeth II). Even so, the tribunal has often faced criticism for giving too much power to the crown to settle claims, and for not providing large enough settlements.

In July 1844, Hone Heke made a symbolic gesture of protest for which he's still remembered, ordering the chopping down of the flagpole in Kororareka that displayed the British flag. Hone Heke later said he made a point of attacking an inanimate symbol of British power rather than harming innocent people, in an expression of his displeasure with how the treaty's terms were playing out. When this flagstaff was replaced, he personally cut it down—twice in January 1845, after which the government sent troops to the area, and again in March.

What followed the troops' arrival became known as the Flagstaff War (or the Northern War). In March 1845, government troops fought Hone Heke and his supporters outside Kororareka. The town was evacuated, and then captured by *pakeha* (white) and pro-British Maori forces. Hone Heke moved inland and set up a *pa*, a type of fortified village with strong defensive positions, and a troop of more than 400 British soldiers followed after him.

Holing up in the pa worked, allowing Hone Heke to fight during the day and stay secure at night. Negotiators offered him several chances to surrender, but he declined them all, and the government attacked the pa on May 8. It launched rockets—a new technology that didn't hit the target—and the pa's defenders were able to retreat during the attack.

Hone Heke's fortunes changed dramatically from there, as he lost two important battles to his main antagonist in the conflict, the pro-British northern chief Tamati Waka Nene.

After the successful defense, Hone Heke left his pa because it had been the site of bloodshed and therefore had become taboo. He moved to another fortified village at Te Ahuahu but, when he and his troops went to get supplies,

SPEAKING THE SAME LANGUAGE

As of the most recent New Zealand census, about one in every seven people in the country identifies as ethnically Maori. While only one in four members of that group speak Maori, the country has taken steps to preserve the language. Since 1987, it has made Maori the co-official language of New Zealand, along with English (and later with sign language), and the national anthem "God Defend New Zealand" opens with a Maori verse followed by an English one. All government buildings and entities have both English and Maori names, and Maori Language Week is a nationwide attempt to keep the language alive. Most famously, the country's world-renowned rugby team, the All Blacks, opens every match with a *haka*, a traditional (and effectively intimidating) Maori battle challenge.

Tamati Waka Nene captured the undefended pa. Hone Heke was shot during the attempt to recapture it, and was forced to sit out fighting for a while. As he recovered from his injury, he wrote letters to government authorities, asking for peace and pointing out that he only fought armies—he had been careful throughout his revolt not to attack towns or civilians (either Maori or pakeha). The only peace offers he received called for his tribe to give up land as part of the terms, which he would not accept, and so the war continued.

Hone Heke's second key loss came at Ruapekapeka, another fortified village controlled by one of his closest allies, Te Ruki Kawiti. The injured chief and his troops weren't able to reach the pa until the bombardment was under way, and this time Hone Heke faced a much larger opposing army. He eventually withdrew and left Ruapekapeka for Nene to capture.

About a week later, Hone Heke and Te Ruki Kawiti met with Nene, under the supervision of a neutral chief. Nene agreed to serve as a go-between for Hone Heke and the new governor in Auckland, George Grey. Eager to put the rebellion behind him, Grey issued a pardon for Hone Heke, Kawiti, and others, and didn't insist on any concessions from the rebels beyond an end to the fighting. Kawiti agreed to Grey's terms right away, but Hone Heke didn't formally surrender until 1848, though he did give up on fighting in the meantime. He lived only about two years after ending his rebellion, dying from tuberculosis on August 7, 1850.

Hone Heke's rebellion later earned the name the First Maori War, as other chiefs fought a series of rebellions against British rule during the next few years. The last of the wars between various iwi and the government ended in 1872, with the crown confiscating more than four million acres of land from tribes that rebelled. ●

ELIZABETH CADY STANTON

THE TIME: *1815–1902*

THE PLACE: *United States*

THE OPPONENT: *Gender inequality*

The movement for American women's voting rights was a long time in the making—so long that Elizabeth Cady Stanton devoted herself to the cause for more than half a century, but still didn't live long enough to see her goal achieved. Without her efforts, however, the movement would have taken even longer.

Born in Johnstown, New York, in 1815, Elizabeth Cady got an outstanding education for a woman of her time. Her father served as a congressman and a judge, encouraged Elizabeth to read law books, and sent her to school at the mixed-gender Johnstown Academy. She studied multiple languages along with writing and science, and attended Troy Female Seminary, since the more prestigious colleges weren't yet open to women.

Elizabeth became active in the abolitionist movement as a young woman, visiting her cousin Gerrit Smith, an active abolitionist who sometimes hosted escaped slaves. (Smith later served as a congressman representing the Free Soil Party, a political party that opposed spreading slavery to new U.S. territories, and was its presidential candidate in 1848). Through him, she met Henry Stanton, an abolitionist and journalist a decade older than her. Not only did he write for famous editors like William Lloyd Garrison and Horace Greeley, but he studied law under his future father-in-law, Daniel Cady.

Elizabeth Cady and Henry Stanton married in 1840, forming an activist power couple. In a sign that she was already thinking about equal rights, Elizabeth removed the traditional phrase "promise to obey" from her wedding service.

In June 1840—as a honeymoon trip—Elizabeth and her husband attended the World's Anti-Slavery Convention in London, which she later credited with

*Elizabeth Cady Stanton holds her daughter
Harriot in an 1856 daguerrotype.*

giving her the idea for a convention for women's rights. The convention spurred
her ideals in two ways: She saw firsthand the power of activists coming together
for a cause, and she experienced discrimination, as female delegates were denied
seats in the convention. The women were eventually seated in a separate section,
where Elizabeth was joined by William Lloyd Garrison (a supporter of equality who chose to sit with the women) and Lucretia Mott (a prominent Quaker
anti-slavery activist who would become a longtime friend and ally).

A few years later, the Stantons moved to the rural town of Seneca Falls, New York. It was there that Elizabeth Cady Stanton (with Lucretia Mott's help) organized the nation's first convention for women's rights. More than 300 people showed up for the two-day Seneca Falls Convention, held July 19–20, 1848. Stanton made the first day's events exclusively for women, but encouraged anyone interested to attend the second day. Quite a few men did, including the legendary abolitionist and escaped slave Frederick Douglass.

Stanton kicked off the two-day event by reading the Declaration of Settlements, a document she wrote based on the Declaration of Independence; it even began in the same way as the earlier document: "When in the course of human events . . ." Just as the founding fathers had itemized ways the king denied Americans their rights, Stanton itemized the rights men had denied to women. Her sixteen-item list included things like the right to vote, the right to a college education, the right to hold most jobs, and the right to get divorced on a woman's terms.

On the convention's second day, 100 delegates (including thirty-two men) signed Stanton's declaration, while the assembly also adopted twelve resolutions calling for specific rights. The only one of the twelve resolutions that didn't pass unanimously? The one calling for women's voting rights. Mott and some other delegates considered that too much, a radical position that would undermine the group's overall goals; even Stanton's mostly progressive husband opposed suffrage while supporting the other ideas. Frederick Douglass spoke up in favor of the resolution, and it did pass, just not unanimously like the other eleven.

Seneca Falls set an important precedent, starting a tradition of annual women's rights conventions where the nation's feminists could meet and coordinate their efforts. Through the declaration, the convention also created a framework for specific laws its attendees could lobby their states to pass.

***

In 1851, Stanton met activist Susan B. Anthony, who was in Seneca Falls to attend an anti-slavery meeting. The two women would become a powerful pair in the fight for equality. Because Stanton's responsibilities as a mother of seven limited her ability to travel—although she did attend events and lecture when she could, and was an excellent speaker—Anthony often served as the movement's public face, reading speeches Stanton wrote.

Most of the leaders of the women's rights movement also remained committed abolitionists, and understandably spent the Civil War years primarily focused on the goal of ending slavery. At the end of the Civil War, however, the women's suffrage movement split over the issue of voting rights for African-Americans. Some prominent leaders, including Elizabeth Cady Stanton and Susan B. Anthony, refused to support the Fourteenth and Fifteenth Amendments to the Constitution, which gave citizenship to former slaves and gave African-American men the right to vote. They argued against endorsing a right for black men but not black (or white) women. An abolitionist senator, Thaddeus Stevens, in 1866 introduced to Congress a petition for universal suffrage, written by suffragettes including Stanton and Anthony. Congress rejected it, and passed the Fourteenth Amendment without expanding the franchise to women.

That split was one reason why *two* national women's organizations formed the same year to advocate similar causes. Stanton and Anthony formed the National Woman Suffrage Association (NWSA) in 1869, while the more conservative American Woman Suffrage Association (AWSA) advanced a similar agenda. By this time, with her children older and requiring less of her attention, Stanton was able to increase her travel schedule. She became one of the most famous women in the United States, advocating for a range of issues that included divorce rights, contraception rights, and voting rights, and even made a run for Congress in 1868 (though she lost).

For the nation's 1876 centennial celebration, Stanton and Matilda Joslyn Gage (another leader in the NWSA) wrote the Declaration of Rights of the Women of the United States, which Anthony read uninvited at the national celebration. The document pointed out again how the principles on which the nation was founded clashed with the second-class status of half its population.

By the time she was in her sixties, Stanton's advocacy efforts mostly consisted of writing, but she remained very active and still traveled around the country and to Europe. In the early 1880s, she co-wrote a multi-volume *History of Women's Suffrage,* along with Matilda Joslyn Gage and Susan B. Anthony. In 1890, her

A PIONEER HONORED

Like Stanton, her longtime friend Susan B. Anthony didn't live quite long enough to see equal voting rights become reality. Anthony, however, received a little more attention and celebrity for her activism. She was honored at the White House on her eightieth birthday, at the invitation of President William McKinley. The first postage stamp with her face was issued in 1936. And in 1979, the United States began issuing dollar coins featuring Anthony, the first woman to appear on American money (at least the first real one, since the Spirit of Liberty appeared in female form). The coins were minted from 1979 to 1981, and then again for a short time in 1999. Knowing that Anthony and Stanton worked so closely together, the Susan B. Anthony coin could be seen as a tribute to Stanton as well, and to all the suffragettes who campaigned for women's rights.

NWSA merged with the AWSA to form one major women's rights organization, and Stanton was elected its president. No fan of organized religion, in 1895 she published *The Women's Bible*, which challenged the Christian traditions that kept women subservient to men (though the book drove a wedge between Stanton and some religious feminists).

In these later years, Stanton achieved a series of victories along the path toward suffrage. Starting with Wyoming in 1890, a handful of western states adopted full voting rights for women, including Colorado, Utah, and Idaho. In 1892, Stanton and a few other prominent suffragettes testified in support of voting rights before the House Judiciary Committee. Her speech was so moving that Lucy Stone—another suffragette who spoke that day—published Stanton's remarks instead of her own in her magazine *Woman's Journal*.

Stanton died of heart failure at eighty-six, on October 26, 1902. It took nearly another eighteen years before her goal of equal voting rights for American women became a reality, a full forty-two years after the amendment to do so was first introduced. What became the Nineteenth Amendment to the Constitution was short and to the point: "The right of citizens of the United States to vote shall not be denied or abridged by the United States or by any State on account of sex. Congress shall have power to enforce this article by appropriate legislation." •

AN IRONIC TRIBUTE

During World War II, the United States named a transport ship the USS *Elizabeth C. Stanton* (or, more accurately, renamed, since it had first been a private commercial ship). The honor was a bit ironic, as Stanton wouldn't have been allowed to join the crew as a full member. The ship was decommissioned shortly after the end of World War II, after taking part in some of the war's most important troop movements, including bringing soldiers to the British Isles ahead of the D-Day invasion of Normandy.

Harriet Tubman ("nurse, spy, and scout," as the original caption describes her) in a poignant photograph taken between 1860 and 1875.

HARRIET TUBMAN

THE TIME: *c. 1820–1913*

THE PLACE: *United States*

THE OPPONENT: *Slavery*

Before the Civil War settled the issue, rebellion against slavery in the American South took many forms. For Harriet Tubman and other members of the Underground Railroad, fighting for freedom meant helping escaped slaves get out of the South and find new lives in the northern United States and in Canada.

The woman known as Harriet Tubman was born Araminta Ross around 1820 on a plantation near Madison, Maryland, where she and her parents were slaves. When she was a young girl, the plantation owners, Edward and Elizabeth Brodess, had her care for other children and rented her out to work on other plantations. They were particularly cruel even when compared to other slave owners, as Tubman described regular lashings even when she was a child. The owners sold three of her sisters, but Harriet's mother managed to stop them from selling her youngest son, threatening to fight until they backed off—a useful lesson for her daughter.

When she was about twelve years old, Araminta suffered a serious injury. While out shopping for supplies, she refused to help restrain a slave who had tried to escape. The man's overseer threw a metal weight at the would-be runaway but hit Araminta in the head instead, causing permanent damage that led to seizures and severe headaches.

Around the same time she sustained her head injury, Araminta became deeply religious. And while she acknowledged that the intense dreams and visions she began to have were caused by the injury, she also considered them religious visions that would guide her path.

After marrying a free black man in the early 1840s, she changed her first name to Harriet (her mother's name) and took her husband's surname of Tub-

A HISTORIC DEDICATION

More than a century after her death, Dorchester County, Maryland, became the home of a Harriet Tubman National Monument, the first national monument celebrating an African-American woman. Fittingly, it was the country's first African-American president, Barack Obama, who called for the establishment of the Tubman Monument on March 25, 2013. The monument includes more than 11,000 acres in the area near where she was born, along the eastern shore of Maryland.

man. Not much is known about her marriage, and like most marriages between free men and slaves, it did nothing to help her become free. She did that on her own.

———————

By 1849, Tubman's health problems had become more serious, which made her plantation owner view her as less of an asset than she had been. When Edward Brodess died, his widow began selling off slaves. Tubman saw what was coming, and knew her family would soon be divided. On September 17, while they were on loan to another plantation, she and her brothers Ben and Henry escaped. Though the two men turned back and returned to the Brodess plantation, Harriet escaped to Pennsylvania, traveling more than ninety miles with the help of a network of slavery opponents.

The Underground Railroad, as that network was known, included a series of safe houses along the way from the South to the North. Escaped slaves could travel between ten and twenty miles overnight, rest at a safe house and get supplies, and then travel to another stop on another night when the coast was clear. There had been previous efforts by abolitionists—those who wanted to outlaw the practice of slavery—to rescue slaves and help them escape north (George Washington was among the owners who lost slaves in this way), but the Underground Railroad had a larger scope and was more thoroughly organized, run by a mix of freed slaves, Quakers (a group that had always opposed slavery), and other abolitionists.

Though there was already a Fugitive Slave Law on the books, which required people to return the runaway slaves they encountered to their owners, Congress passed a much stricter one in September 1850. Northern states had found several ways around the old law, and the new one (part of the Compromise of 1850 that also divided potential states like Texas and California into slave or free states) closed those loopholes. Essentially, it required Northern states where slavery was illegal to enforce Southern laws when it came to the newly free—with fines or jail time for anyone who fed or housed escaped slaves. Though plenty of Northerners refused to comply, the law made all blacks in the North targets. Capturing escaped slaves brought advertised rewards, and many free blacks were captured and sold into slavery, unable to do much to correct the situation.

A few months after that law passed, Tubman began the first of her runs as a "conductor" on the Underground Railroad, returning to Maryland to rescue her niece and her niece's children from a slave auction. She went on to carry out more expeditions and rescue more family members—including both of her parents as well as several siblings—and eventually anyone she could help free.

———————

In her decade serving as a conductor, Harriet Tubman made nineteen trips back to the South, personally helping dozens of slaves (the oft-quoted figure of 300 is probably inflated, but it was a still a large number). Her conductor trips were incredibly risky, the equivalent of an undercover mission deep in enemy territory. The combination of her heroic actions and her religious perspective caused the abolitionist newspaper publisher William Lloyd Garrison to give Tubman the nickname "Moses."

She was a brilliant strategist who developed an effective system for smuggling slaves to freedom. For example, she did a lot of her conducting on Saturdays, specifically because most newspapers wouldn't be able to run escaped-slave ads until Monday, buying her an extra day to get them to safety. She varied her routes, making sure her patterns didn't become predictable if anyone came looking for her. Though she became a famous resistance figure and large rewards were offered for her capture, Tubman was never caught—and neither were any of the slaves she conducted to freedom. As she once said, "I never ran my train off the track and I never lost a passenger."

In all, thousands of slaves used the Underground Railroad to escape to the North over two decades—depending on which estimates are right, anywhere from 6,000 to 30,000. Ontario, Canada—still a British colony—was the most popular destination, since slavery was fully illegal there, while even free Northern states were affected by the Fugitive Slave Law.

A celebrity among abolitionists, Harriet Tubman gave speeches to supportive crowds and even helped recruit volunteers for John Brown's anti-slavery raids (see page 113). She made her last conductor trip in December 1860, though other conductors continued to make Underground Railroad runs.

———————

When the Civil War began, Harriet Tubman found new ways to serve the abolitionist cause. She worked as a nurse and cook, primarily in South Carolina, where abolitionist general David Hunter was organizing a regiment of freed slaves to fight for the Union. She also carried out spying raids in the area, applying the undercover skills she'd used on her conducting trips. In June 1863, she became the first woman to lead an armed assault during the war. She led

A QUESTION OF VALUE

There is a famous story that Tubman's importance to the anti-slavery cause resulted in a $40,000 offered reward for her capture. But the story is probably untrue, since $40,000 was an astronomical amount of money at the time—millions of dollars in today's money—at a time when the South was hurting financially. The tale probably dates to the 1867 effort to get Harriet Tubman a full Civil War pension, when her supporters were highlighting her importance to the cause. Some historians, however, have suggested the figure was a cumulative total of all the rewards offered by various parties who wanted to get her out of the picture.

one of two ships that traveled upriver to Combahee Ferry, South Carolina, to free the area's slaves, and rescued hundreds by ship. The Combahee Ferry Raid worked well enough that the Union used the same tactic elsewhere—freeing slaves, recruiting supporters and soldiers among the rescued, and denying the Confederacy unpaid labor.

After the war ended and slavery was abolished, Harriet Tubman returned to Auburn, New York, where she and her family had moved in 1859, living on land she bought at a discount from an abolitionist senator. She spent the last years of her life in a rest home for the elderly, named in her honor, on land she donated to an African-American church. She died of pneumonia in 1913, not long after enduring brain surgery to try to relieve worsening symptoms of the head injury she'd lived with since childhood. ●

GERONIMO

THE TIME: *1829–1909*

THE PLACE: *Apache territory*

THE OPPONENTS: *Mexico, United States*

With his history of raiding enemies, eluding capture, and escaping imprisonment, the Apache leader Geronimo became a kind of outlaw celebrity. To fans, he was a renegade freedom fighter who refused to bow to those invading Apache land. To the governments of Mexico and the United States, he was a terrorist threat.

Geronimo was born in 1829, near the Gila River in what is now New Mexico. At the time, the area where the Apache tribes lived was occupied by Mexico, which had recently fought a war of independence against Spain. The Apache included several related peoples, and Geronimo was a member of the Chiricahua tribe (today known as the Fort Sill Apache), and within it the Bedonkohe band.

He was originally named Goyakla ("he who yawns"), and was married when he was seventeen. At the time, the Apache tribes raided their neighbors for supplies, and in 1835 the Mexican government in the state of Sonora (where Geronimo's band lived) responded by paying bounty hunters for every Apache scalp they collected, even those of young children. This policy meant Geronimo and his band were often on the run, hunted for crimes which they had nothing to do with.

While Geronimo and many other men were away on a trading trip in March 1851, a Mexican army attacked his camp. When the men returned, they found their camp and supplies destroyed, their horses stolen, and many of their family members dead. The murdered included all of Geronimo's family—his mother, his wife, and all three of his young children.

At the time, Geronimo's band of the Chiricahua had been technically at peace with Mexico, but the murders ensured Geronimo would hold a lifelong vendetta against the state; even in old age, he believed the murders justified hatred of all Mexicans. In his grief, the twenty-one-year-old Geronimo organized a troop of 200 Apache men to hunt and kill the Mexican soldiers who had killed their families. The nickname "Geronimo," by which he would be known the rest of his life, was born in one particular battle against Mexican forces about a year after his family members' deaths—supposedly, his enemies called out for the help of St. Jerome, and received only Geronimo's brand of justice.

———

It turned out that the land where Geronimo and his band were living wasn't even under Mexican control at the time of his family's massacre. In 1848, the Treaty of Guadalupe Hidalgo ended the Mexican-American War, and the terms included Mexico ceding much of the Southwest—including most Apache territory—to the United States. While he already had reason to hate Mexico, Geronimo soon had reason to hate the United States, as large numbers of Americans began snapping up Apache land.

As more Americans settled in the territories gained by the Mexican Cession, they began to mine the area, establish large ranches, and build towns. The settlements pushed Apache bands out of their ancestral land and restricted their movements, after they had been accustomed to having free reign throughout the area.

While Geronimo made a point of raiding and terrorizing Mexican settlements in the area for more than a decade as part of his ongoing mission of revenge, his band also did the same to ranches and villages built by these American newcomers. As more Americans headed west, more of their vehicles and wagon trains were raided by Apaches, sometimes in violent surprise attacks.

———

In 1872, the Apache, like many other Native American peoples before and after them, were ordered onto a reservation by the United States government. Initially, the reservation was local, allowing the Chiricahua Apaches to at least live on

Geronimo homes in on the viewer in a photograph from 1904.

part of their ancestral land. Their leader, Cochise (who was the remarried Geronimo's father-in-law), agreed to a peace deal with the Americans that included resettlement on that reservation. Geronimo apparently disagreed with the decision, but still complied with it.

However, the arrangement lasted only a few years before the federal government forced the Chiricahua to move again. In this case, the government saw Cochise's death as an excuse to move his tribe to the San Carlos Reservation in eastern Arizona, where the government had moved other Apache tribes but which had no connection to Chiricahua land.

Geronimo saw San Carlos as nothing short of a prison, and organized small groups of followers in a series of prison breaks. When relocation began, he escaped to Mexico with a small team, but they were captured and brought back to San Carlos. He led another escape a few years later, carrying out raids from a base in the Sierra Madre Mountains before being arrested again.

In 1885, Geronimo attempted yet another escape from the reservation. This time, he and his small troop of thirty-eight Apaches (including women and children) managed to avoid capture for more than a year. They traveled throughout the southwestern United States, carrying out raids to survive and sometimes killing Americans or Mexicans. Newspaper coverage of some of those killings only made Geronimo more famous, and put pressure on the Feds to bring him back to the reservation.

That effort to capture Geronimo ultimately took about 5,000 United States soldiers under the command of veteran "Indian hunter" General Nelson A. Miles, backed by about 5,000 more Mexican troops. Eventually, his time on the run took its toll on Geronimo. When Miles and his men caught up to the Apache fugitives near the Arizona-Mexico border, Geronimo met with the general and agreed to surrender in exchange for a short sentence (a deal the army later claimed it didn't make, and which Geronimo accused them of lying about).

SKULL AND BONES

A century after his death, the whereabouts of Geronimo's skull sparked a controversy. In February 2009, twenty of his descendants filed a lawsuit against several parties—including the federal government—asking for its return. The complaint concerned Skull and Bones, a famous secret society of current and former Yale University students. Legend has it that Skull and Bones members (among them Prescott Bush, father and grandfather of future presidents George H. W. and George W. Bush) stole Geronimo's skull in 1918 and made it part of the group's ceremonies. Since Skull and Bones keeps all its activities secret from non-members, the group has never confirmed that rumor, and the lawsuit was dismissed for lack of evidence.

GERONIMO!!!

The name "Geronimo" has become a common saying (or, more accurately, screaming) among people jumping out of airplanes. Supposedly, the practice dates to a 1940 army parachuting trial at Fort Benning, Georgia, when a private said he would yell "Geronimo" (his friends had just seen a movie about the Apache leader) to show he wasn't scared when jumping. He did, and the expression caught on, becoming a kind of unofficial slogan for military and civilian skydivers and parachutists.

After their surrender on September 4, 1886, Geronimo and his supporters—who by this point included about 400 Apaches—were sent to reservations in Florida, with the men separated from the women and children. Geronimo was moved several times, and spent the last fourteen years of his life at Fort Sill, Oklahoma, on a reservation far away from his people's land.

In all, Geronimo spent his last twenty-seven years classified as a prisoner of war, a famous living example of the defeat of the Native Americans in the last round of "Indian Wars" with the United States. Late in life, the Apache leader dictated his autobiography, meeting regularly with a school superintendent named S. M. Barrett to tell his story, which was published only with the permission of President Theodore Roosevelt. He also became a sought-after celebrity, appearing at the 1904 World's Fair in St. Louis and drawing crowds seeking photographs with the famous warrior.

Geronimo lived to be seventy-nine, dying of pneumonia on February 17, 1909. A few days earlier, he'd been thrown from his horse, and he became sick while wounded on the ground overnight. As his last words, he is said to have told his nephew, "I should have never surrendered. I should have fought until I was the last man alive." •

SITTING BULL

THE TIME: *c. 1831–1890*

THE PLACE: *Sioux territory*

THE OPPONENT: *United States*

By the time Sitting Bull became the head chief of his faction of the Lakota Sioux, the United States government had a long history of making deals with Native American nations, only to change the terms when they proved inconvenient. When that happened on his watch, Sitting Bull rallied the Sioux together in a historic last stand.

The son of a respected warrior, Sitting Bull was born about 1831, in what was then the Dakota Territory. His birth name was actually Hoka Psice (Jumping Badger), and as a young man he established himself as a religious and military figure among the Hunkpapa Lakota, one of several Sioux nations based in the Dakotas and Montana. When he was fourteen, he earned his new name, Tatanka-Yotanka (a name describing a seated, unmovable buffalo bull), by proving himself in a raid against the Crow.

When it came to his attitude toward the United States, Sitting Bull was essentially a separatist, wanting his people to live their traditional ways on their traditional land, with minimal interference from the always-expanding country around them. In practice, that meant armed opposition to one incursion after another.

In 1862, some Santee Sioux—a different Sioux people also called the Eastern Dakota—had responded to a series of treaty violations by carrying out several attacks against white settlers in western Minnesota and reportedly killing more than 800 people. When the army sent brigades to Dakota to retaliate, however, it also attacked Sioux villages and people who hadn't had anything to do with

TAKING THE SHOW ON THE ROAD

Late in life, Sitting Bull became something of an entertainment celebrity. In 1885, looking to earn extra money and do what he could to improve white attitudes toward his people, Sitting Bull sought permission from the federal government to leave the reservation and spend a few months with Buffalo Bill Cody's touring Wild West Show.

He met the famous sharpshooter Annie Oakley on tour, and the two became so close that Sitting Bull adopted her as a daughter. He also posed for a famous picture with then-president Grover Cleveland. However, he was booed at some stops along the tour, and there were rumors at the time that he cursed audiences in Lakota (though that might have just been one of Cody's ploys to make Sitting Bull appear exotic). Sitting Bull wound up leaving the tour early, and the government denied him permission to return the following year. Still, he was a popular draw and made about $50 per week (good money at the time), plus whatever he charged for autographs or photographs.

the incident—including the Hunkpapa Lakota.

Sitting Bull fought white Americans for the first time during these attacks. He was among those who led an unsuccessful pan-Sioux defense at the Battle of Killdeer Mountain in July 1864, when Brigadier General Alfred Sully led 2,200 men into Dakota as part of the same campaign.

Santee Sioux fleeing west told Sitting Bull and other Lakota about what life was like on federal Indian reservations. Their stories about the lack of freedom and the poor conditions hardened Sitting Bull's resolve never to sign any treaty that would move his people to a reservation, and to fight in defense of Lakota land rights. When the Ogala Lakota chief Red Cloud took on the United States Army, Sitting Bull joined the fight by leading war parties on Red Cloud's behalf.

Red Cloud ended his war by treaty in 1868, agreeing to move his people to a large reservation, but Sitting Bull and his tribe didn't sign. That same year, Sitting Bull became chief of the Hunkpapa Lakota, and continued to carry out guerilla-style raids against white settlers encroaching on Lakota territory—even managing to drive out a survey party that was trying to establish a route for the Northern Pacific Railroad.

Not surprisingly, money became a motive for the United States to threaten Lakota territory again, in the process setting off war with Sitting Bull. In 1874, gold was discovered in the Black Hills, prompting a rush of prospectors looking to make their fortune there. The gold deposits had been found by an army officer, George Armstrong Custer, who was also looking for a spot to establish a military base.

The land in question was theoretically protected under the 1868 Fort Laramie Treaty, which gave the Lakota full dominion over the Black Hills. Wanting the access to gold at a time when the United States had just suffered a huge financial panic, the government tried buying the land from the Lakota, who refused. Delegations of different Sioux tribes met with President Ulysses S. Grant and other leaders in Washington in May 1875, but every new American treaty proposal involved moving the Sioux from their land to reservations. The idea of a peaceful solution seemed unlikely.

The final straw for Sitting Bull came when Edward Smith, the federal commissioner of Indian Affairs, invalidated the existing treaty and announced that any Lakota who had not moved to reservations by January 31, 1876, would be considered hostile and fair game for attack.

Sitting Bull knew that attack was coming and, as three columns of federal troops arrived in March 1876, he called together local Lakota, Cheyenne, and Arapaho to form an alliance against the encroaching military.

Despite his own military credentials, Sitting Bull didn't lead troops in what would be called the Great Sioux War of 1876. Instead, he served as a spiritual leader and a big-picture strategist. While holding a religious ceremony for the combined nations at his camp, he slashed his own arms 100 times to demonstrate his commitment to the cause. He also told the assembly of a vision he'd had, in which he saw soldiers and horses falling from the sky upside down. He declared it a sign that the united tribes would defeat the coming invasion.

Sitting Bull's supporters won a quick victory at the Battle of the Rosebud on June 17, under the leadership of Crazy Horse, who surprised one of the three federal columns in Montana Territory and drove them away. That allowed Sitting Bull to relocate his growing camp, setting up near the Little Bighorn River.

George Custer, whose gold-seeking expedition had started the whole conflict, was now in command of the Seventh Cavalry. On June 25, 1876, badly underestimating how many men Sitting Bull had in camp, Custer attacked. Sitting Bull's troops, number-

Sitting Bull sits bullishly in this portrait from 1885.

A MAN OF VISIONS

Just as Sitting Bull was said to have a vision of his people defeating the army of George Custer, he reported seeing a prophetic vision about his own death. A few years before he died, after he was already back in Standing Rock, he saw a meadowlark that supposedly warned him, "Your own people, Lakotas, will kill you." Which was true, in the sense that the police were themselves Lakota, though operating under American orders.

ing as many as 2,000, were able to fend off Custer and his 262 cavalrymen. Custer had no choice but to retreat and attempt a last stand on a nearby mountain ridge, where his entire detachment was killed by warriors from the combined tribes.

The defeat of Custer's troops at Little Bighorn was a huge shock to the United States, but they dug in. Waves of cavalry invaded Sioux and Cheyenne territory, forcing one chief after another to submit to federal rule.

Sitting Bull and a band of supporters fled to Canada in 1877 and lived in exile there for about four years, but he eventually found it too difficult to feed his people. On July 19, 1881, Sitting Bull had no choice but to return to Montana and surrender. Federal authorities held him and some of his followers as prisoners of war for nearly two years, before moving them to the Standing Rock reservation in what's now North Dakota.

Despite his surrender, Sitting Bull was still seen as a respected spiritual leader on the reservation, and therefore viewed as a threat by the government. In 1890, a religious movement known as the Ghost Dance was growing among the Lakota. This movement was based on the idea that the practice of certain rituals could drive white settlers from the area and restore Sioux sovereignty.

On December 15, 1890, Sitting Bull was killed in a shoot-out with police. With the Ghost Dance becoming a threat, the authorities on the Standing Rock reservation had decided to arrest him before he joined the movement. In the early morning, forty-three Lakota police officers entered Sitting Bull's cabin and dragged him outside to arrest him, while supporters heard what was happening and tried to protect him. The standoff turned into a shoot-out, and an officer named Bullhead shot the legendary chief in the head. Fourteen people died in the skirmish.

The killing of Sitting Bull only strengthened Sioux interest in the Ghost Dance. Two weeks after his death, the United States army opened fire on a Lakota reservation at Wounded Knee, South Dakota. As many as 350 Lakota, including women and children, were killed at the Wounded Knee Massacre, which effectively ended the Sioux opposition movement Sitting Bull had helped lead. •

MARY HARRIS JONES

THE TIME: *c. 1837–1930*

THE PLACE: *United States*

THE OPPONENT: *Unfair labor practices*

Members of the American working class in the late 1800s and early 1900s had a radically different experience than American workers of today. Many of the conditions Americans now take for granted, from eight-hour workdays to basic safety standards, grew out of the labor movement of that era, and Mary Harris "Mother" Jones ranks among that movement's most important figures.

Mary Harris was born in Cork, Ireland, sometime between 1830 and 1840 (she never knew for sure), and the early years of her life were filled with hardship. Her birth coincided with the Great Famine of Ireland, when the country's potato crop suddenly failed. About a million people died, and another million—including the Harris family—left Ireland in order to escape starvation. Her parents settled in Toronto, Canada, where Mary was educated before moving to Michigan to work as a teacher.

She later moved to Chicago and then to Memphis, Tennessee, where she married a union ironworker named George Jones in 1861. The couple had four children in less than six years, but tragedy soon struck the young family.

Mother Jones certainly knew how to pose for a photo.

In 1867, Memphis experienced its second of four massive outbreaks of yellow fever, a deadly disease carried by mosquitoes. Many died, including Mary's husband and all four of her children. From this time on, Mary Harris Jones wore black every day as part of her lifelong mourning, and her black dresses would eventually become an iconic part of her image. She never remarried or had more children.

As a widow in her thirties or forties, Jones had no reason to stay in Memphis, so she moved back to Chicago and started a dressmaking business. Tragedy struck again, as the Great Chicago Fire of 1871 destroyed her shop, her home, and all the possessions she had left.

With no family, no job, and no home, Mary Harris Jones chose to devote her time and energy to the emerging union movement. Her dressmaking work had put her in contact with many wealthy clients, and she later wrote that seeing their indifference to the circumstances of working people energized her to get involved in labor struggles.

Since the start of the Industrial Revolution a few decades earlier, the United States had begun to dramatically shift from an agricultural economy to an industrial one, with more people moving to cities for work. With many more available workers than jobs—and with the government imposing few regulations on the fast-growing industries—companies easily took advantage of their employees. Unions gave workers the chance to bargain and make demands as a group, and they became a more important tool for workers than they ever had before. Because of the power they afforded workers, unions were generally very unpopular with business owners, and bosses often responded with violence, hiring strikebreakers or even getting governors to send troops to intimidate, beat, or kill workers who demanded better conditions.

For several years, Jones was something of a nomad, traveling around the country from one strike to another, as she gave speeches and did what she could to help unions organize. Much of her early activism involved a fledgling organization called the Knights of Labor, whose agenda included pushing for an eight-hour workday and an end to convict and child labor. An outstanding speaker and charismatic leader, she helped inspire workers during an 1877 railroad strike in Pittsburgh and soon did the same for striking workers in a variety of industries and cities.

Though Knights of Labor membership had reached about 700,000 workers by 1886, it declined after that year's Haymarket Riots, in which Chicago workers striking for an eight-hour workday clashed with police. After that, Jones shifted much of her focus to helping miners, joining up with the young United Mine Workers union and helping it gain thirty times its original membership in

MOTHER OF ALL MAGAZINES

In 1976, three former staffers of the defunct progressive magazine *Ramparts* founded a new progressive magazine in San Francisco, and named it *Mother Jones* in honor of the labor leader. The non-profit magazine, which covers politics and current affairs, is known for its investigative journalism and has won six National Magazine Awards.

just a few years. She earned the nickname "the Miners' Angel" for her presence marching alongside strikers and looking out for their interests.

By the end of the century, she was known by another nickname, "Mother Jones," and served as a female authority figure for thousands of miners. She showed up to rallies in a uniform of sorts, wearing her trademark black dress, a lace collar, and an elaborate hat. Jones started exaggerating her age to make herself seem older, and her maternal persona soon made her famous across the country. With her rallying cry of "pray for the dead and fight like hell for the living," she was able to bring attention to often-ignored issues, thanks to her fame. In 1902, a district attorney in West Virginia called Jones "the most dangerous woman in America," crediting her with the ability to make hundreds of men walk off the job with one speech.

Mother Jones's efforts went far beyond the rights of mine and railroad workers, and she helped organize everyone from garment workers to mill employees to transportation operators—any group she felt was being exploited by their bosses. (Though the women's suffrage movement was active at the same time, Jones took little interest in it and did not consider herself a feminist, focusing on issues of class rather than gender.) She also helped found the Industrial Workers of the World (she was the only woman among its original signatories), raised money for labor causes, and toured the country as a lecturer and union advocate.

In 1903, Jones organized a "Children's Crusade" to protest child labor. Starting in Philadelphia, she led a group of about 100 children to President Theodore Roosevelt's Long Island summer home. Her procession included several kids with severe injuries acquired on the job, at a time when employers didn't pay for medical care. The president refused to meet with the children, but the march raised awareness of the problems of child labor, as she stopped in towns along the way to speak with locals and get newspapers to cover the issue.

BIRTHDAY WISHES

Mother Jones didn't know the full details of when she was born, or even how old she was, so she decided to make it all up. Though baptism records (discovered later) list her birthday as August 1, 1837, late in life she decided to celebrate her birthday as May 1, 1830. May 1 had already become an international labor holiday, with May Day ceremonies held around the world to commemorate the 1886 Haymarket Riots in Chicago. She chose 1830 as her birth year so that her 1930 birthday celebration could be considered a centennial, though she was probably only in her early nineties.

Jones not only didn't fear arrest or jail, but saw them as ways to bring attention to injustice and therefore effect change. She was arrested multiple times while helping miners strike in Colorado. West Virginia put her under house arrest for more than two months in 1913 on charges of inciting a riot during a coal workers' strike—until public pressure forced the governor to release her. When a critic in the United States Senate called her "the grandmother of all agitators," she responded that she hoped to live long enough to be considered the great-grandmother instead.

In one of her biggest victories, Jones persuaded industrial giant John D. Rockefeller to meet with her after the 1914 Ludlow Massacre, in which the National Guard murdered two dozen people during a miners' strike, including women and children. The massacre brought attention to the ongoing problem of violence against strikers, and that attention spurred Rockefeller to agree to better working conditions in his mines.

Though it's often (and correctly) said that she lost more battles than she won, that wasn't unusual for the labor movement, which was always the underdog to the richest men in America. What she and other labor organizers did was advance the conversation around labor, fighting for better conditions across industries and gradually winning small victories that eventually resulted in a very different American workplace.

Jones left the United Mine Workers in the 1920s, but remained active in labor causes. Her last strike appearance, in 1924, brought her full circle, as she supported dressmakers in Chicago. (That one didn't go so well—hundreds of strikers were blacklisted, and the publisher of the *Chicago Tribune* won a large defamation suit against Jones.) The following year, she wrote *The Autobiography of Mother Jones*, a popular book that detailed her five decades as an activist and self-described "hellraiser."

She eventually retired to a friend's farm in Maryland, and died in Silver Springs in 1930. Per her instructions, she was buried in Mount Olive, Illinois, in a cemetery for union coal miners. At her funeral, the priest described her as nothing less than "the Joan of Arc of labor." ●

LILIUOKALANI

THE TIME: *1838–1917*

THE PLACE: *Hawaii*

THE OPPONENT: *United States*

Discontent with simply controlling a nation that stretched from the Atlantic to the Pacific Oceans, by the late 1800s some American interests began looking to the Pacific itself as a source of more land and more commerce. That search included Hawaii, whose last queen did what she could to oppose the United States taking over the islands. Overthrown in an American-backed coup, she tried a last-ditch counterrevolution, but came up short.

Liliuokalani (the royal name she received once heir to the throne) was born Lydia Kamakaeha in the city of Honolulu in 1838. Her father, Kaisera Kapaakea, was a high chief who served in the kingdom's legislature (the House of Nobles) from 1845 until his death. Her mother, Analea Keohokalole, was a high chieftess and also part of the ruling Kalakaua line. Their status made Liliuokalani a princess, and she received a missionary education that left her fluent in English.

Hawaii was still a fairly young kingdom at the time of Liliuokalani's birth. Kamehameha I had unified the islands and chiefs of Hawaii in 1801 after a fifteen-year war, in which he relied on Western advisors and weapons. His victory created a monarchy along with a legislature that included chiefs from all the islands, but with the monarch holding considerable power.

While the future queen was still a child, Hawaii became one of the first non-European nations to receive full recognition from other world powers. In 1843, Great Britain and France issued a joint proclamation recognizing Hawaii's independence. This was an important step, as those two nations had each had run-ins with the Hawaiian government and (along with Germany) were starting to claim more territory in the Pacific. The United States refused to join the statement, though it later recognized Hawaii as a nation in 1849. The international recognition meant the Kingdom of Hawaii could set up consulates around the world, and have formal diplomatic relations.

In February 1874, Liliuokalani's older brother, Kalakaua, became king (elected by the legislature when the previous king died heirless), and named their brother William Pitt Leleiohoku next in line as his heir. William died just three years later, making Liliuokalani heir apparent to King Kalakaua. She served as regent when the king went on a world tour in 1881, and took her own world tour in 1887. As a representative of her nation at the Queen's Jubilee in London, she met with leaders like Queen Victoria and President Grover Cleveland.

Unfortunately for Liliuokalani, at the same time the queen was making connections outside the islands, a group of non-native subjects inside her territory was plotting her family's overthrow. With an armed militia at their back, in 1887 a team of mostly American businessmen forced King Kalakaua to sign what became known as the "Bayonet Constitution." Among other things, it greatly limited the number of people who were eligible to vote in Hawaii. Asians lost that power completely, and all other voters were required to own a minimum amount of land (although non-citizen residents from the United States were allowed to vote). The Bayonet Constitution also included a treaty that gave the United States control of the strategically important Pearl Harbor, and a number of unique advantages when it came to trade.

Liliuokalani vocally opposed the Bayonet Constitution, as it made the monarchy a lot weaker and the cabal of American businessmen based in Hawaii a lot stronger. When her brother died in January 1891, Liliuokalani became queen, and the first sole female ruler of Hawaii. She openly planned to get rid of the new

Liliuokalani, pacifically, c. 1915.

STILL UNDER FOREIGN RULE

While Hawaii voted for statehood, the United States still holds Guam, American Samoa, and the Northern Mariana Islands as territories—using Guam in particular as a large military base, where nearly 30 percent of the land has been taken over by military installations. While most of the other Pacific Islands are now parts of independent nations, a few remain colonies. France continues to rule French Polynesia, Tahiti, New Caledonia, and Wallis and Futuna. The remote Rapa Nui (also called Easter Island) remains under the control of Chile, which annexed it in 1888.

constitution, which angered the powerful men who'd created it in the first place. They didn't give her time to make that change.

On January 16, 1893, a group of American marines invaded Hawaii. Liliuokalani surrendered the throne at gunpoint, in an effort to avoid violence. The invasion was led by Sanford B. Dole, a cousin of the man who would later found the Dole Fruit Company to export Hawaiian pineapple. Previously a justice under Kalakaua, Dole was chosen president of a new provisional government. The coup leaders later declared a Republic of Hawaii (and negotiated recognition for it with foreign governments), but their plan was always to have the United States eventually annex Hawaii.

Using the political connections she'd gained years earlier, Liliuokalani appealed to President Cleveland for help. He listened and considered the matter, appointing former congressman (and annexation opponent) James Blount to conduct a full investigation. Blount's July 1893 report placed the blame squarely on forces within the United States—specifically, the business leaders who planned the coup and the members of the navy and marines who had carried it out. The report also branded the coup illegitimate, illegal, and a violation of international law.

Cleveland offered to help reinstall Liliuokalani as ruler of Hawaii, but on the condition that the men involved in the coup would receive amnesty. She initially rejected that idea, and by the time she changed her mind, the coup leaders were more firmly in power and rejected Cleveland's attempts to return the queen to power.

She tried a different approach to regain control of Hawaii in 1895, backing a rebellion led by Robert Wilcox, a pro-monarchy native Hawaiian. Wilcox had organized a rebellion against her brother Kalakaua after the signing of the Bayonet Constitution, and joined other conspirators in planning a military strategy of their own to bring Liliuokalani back to power.

A MUSICAL LEGACY

If being queen wasn't enough of an achievement, Liliuokalani also ranks as arguably the most important composer of Hawaiian music, having written more than 100 songs. One of her works, "Aloha Oe," might be the most recognizable Hawaiian song ever composed, recorded by the likes of Elvis Presley and Johnny Cash, and serving as the basis for a short story by Jack London. She played a variety of musical instruments—from the ukulele to the zither—and was also the first Hawaiian woman to publish a book, telling the story of her reign and overthrow in *Hawaii's Story by Hawaii's Queen.*

The Wilcox-led rebellion, however, fell apart quickly. Starting with a two-day clash at Diamond Head, loyalist troops fought coup-backed forces at a series of battles in early January. Wilcox and the other leaders were captured, and sentenced to death for treason. The coup leaders also placed Liliuokalani under house arrest when a cache of weapons was found on her property (she denied knowing about them). On January 24, 1895, she signed a formal abdication, giving up her claim on the throne in exchange for pardons for herself, Wilcox, and the other rebels. She continued to oppose annexation, speaking out as part of a protest movement called *Oni pa'a* (Stand Firm).

After the U.S. presidential election of 1896, the Democratic president Cleveland was replaced by Republican William McKinley, who supported the annexation of Hawaii and ended any hopes Liliuokalani still had of restoring her monarchy, or even just maintaining Hawaii's independence. In July 1898, McKinley's administration made annexation official; the nation of Hawaii was a thing of the past.

The United States didn't end its colonial ambitions in the Pacific with Hawaii. The next month, it won the Spanish-American War that had begun in April 1898, claiming Guam and the Philippines as territories (as well as Cuba and Puerto Rico).

Liliuokalani remained in Hawaii, where she died of a stroke on November 11, 1917, her former nation still an official United States territory. It remained so for decades, listed as a non-self-governing territory by the United Nations after World War II. In 1959, President Dwight Eisenhower signed a bill allowing Hawaiians to vote for statehood. The statehood measure passed with about 93 percent of the vote, though only about a quarter of Hawaii's population voted. On August 21, 1959, Hawaii became the fiftieth member of the United States. ●

KATE SHEPPARD

THE TIME: *1847–1934*

THE PLACE: *New Zealand*

THE OPPONENT: *Gender inequality*

Not that long ago, even the most democratic of the world's democratic countries allowed only half their adult populations to vote. New Zealand became the first country in modern times where women gained that fundamental right, but it didn't happen overnight. Nobody played a bigger role in that successful fight for voting rights than Kate Sheppard.

Catherine Malcolm (she changed the spelling of her first name later) was born in Liverpool, England, in 1847, though she spent a good deal of her childhood in Scotland. After her father died, her mother moved with twenty-one-year-old Kate and Kate's three siblings from Great Britain to Christchurch, the largest city on the South Island of New Zealand.

She married a local shopkeeper named Walter Sheppard in 1871, and became a housewife and mother. Kate Sheppard was active in the Trinity Congregationalist Church and in early temperance organizations—groups that campaigned for the banning of alcohol—and even then advocated a greater role for women in society. She wasn't alone. By the 1870s, women's suffrage movements were gaining traction in much of the English-speaking world. Though most weren't able to get voting laws passed, they did introduce the issue into the national conversation. (In New Zealand, women could already vote in two parts of the country—Otago and Nelson—but only if they owned property and paid taxes, so this mostly applied to widows.)

While in her late thirties, Sheppard became a much more active activist. In 1885, she co-founded the New Zealand chapter of the Women's Christian Temperance Union (WCTU), which had started in the United States eleven years earlier. As an early New Zealand feminist, Sheppard took stands beyond the temperance movement. She argued against corsets and other popular fashions that altered the shape of women's bodies. At a time when women were expected to be fragile, she was one of the first Kiwi women to take up cycling, and advocated for fitness instead of frailty. These kinds of arguments gained traction in New Zealand, where a farm-based economy and a desire for something more democratic than Great Britain's rigid class structure made more people open to women leading active lives.

Temperance movements worldwide tended to have female leaders, with prevailing ideas of the era suggesting that women were more morally pure than men. However, the same notion was used to keep women out of "dirty" business, like politics and legal matters. Sheppard was more than willing to take on such issues, using her position in the Temperance Union to speak up for women's rights when it came to contraception, divorce, custody of children, and employment opportunities.

While the WCTU began around the idea of limiting access to alcohol and other perceived social ills, Sheppard and other leaders felt the women's temperance movement would become far more effective if women actually had a say in the government. Almost from the WCTU's start, Sheppard pushed voting rights as the key to opening government to the rest of the feminist movement's ideas.

In addition to being an inspiring leader, Kate Sheppard was also a good writer and used that skill to rally the public, as an editor and writer for the *Prohibitionist* (the temperance movement's national newspaper) and a writer of short pamphlets on feminist issues. Her 1888 pamphlet *Ten Reasons Why the Women*

PIONEERS IN POLITICS

Though New Zealand women could vote starting in 1893, the country didn't get its first female prime minister until December 1997. Jenny Shipley wasn't elected—she replaced the sitting prime minister, Jim Bolger, within the National Party—but she served as the country's thirty-sixth prime minister until 1999. She lost her first election for a full term, but her opponent was Labour Party leader Helen Clark, who became the first *elected* female prime minister of New Zealand. Clark won two more terms, serving nearly nine years before Labour lost to National in 2008 and John Key replaced her.

of N.Z. Should Vote not only made effective arguments, but showed Sheppard had the dry wit and logical approach to win over skeptics. (One of her ten reasons? "Because it has not yet been proved that the intelligence of women is only equal to that of children, nor that their social status is on par with that of lunatics or convicts.") She sent the document to numerous members of the New Zealand Parliament, but it didn't spur them to action.

Sheppard and the WCTU began collecting signatures from women around the country, planning to petition Parliament to give women the right to vote. The first attempt, in 1891, gained more than 9,000 signatures and the support of

Kate Sheppard sits still just long enough for her photo to be taken in 1905.

some prominent members of Parliament, including John Hall, Alfred Saunders, and the country's highest-ranking official, Premier John Ballance. Even with their support, however, the effort wasn't enough. They tried again the following year, more than doubling the total to 19,000 signatures. Again, it wasn't enough to sway Parliament.

The WCTU would not be stopped. In 1893, it circulated another petition, which became the largest in New Zealand history to that point, with more than 32,000 signatures (at the time, representing about one of every three women in the country) collected by an organization numbering some 600 members. With that kind of public support, suffrage backer John Hall had the leverage to get Parliament to finally take up the issue.

Ballance, another valuable ally, had died in office and been replaced as premier by Richard Seddon, who wasn't yet willing to sign off on voting rights for women. The growing support for suffrage terrified the liquor industry because of the movement's connection to temperance, and it organized its own (less successful) anti-suffrage petition drives in pubs. Pressure from his party eventually forced Seddon to introduce a bill that allowed equal voting rights and, though he tried maneuvering to block its passage, the measure passed in a close vote.

Sheppard achieved her primary goal with the passage of the Electoral Act 1893 by both houses of Parliament, and it became law on September 19. Suffrage went into effect before the nation's election that November, with all women twenty-one and over able to participate, including the indigenous Maori

FIRST AND LASTING

While New Zealand takes pride in being the first modern nation where women had the right to vote, it's slightly more accurate to say it was the first to give *all* women the right to vote and never take it away. Women could vote in Sweden from 1717 to 1781, but only if they were tax-paying members of certain guilds. For short times, Poland and Finland allowed women to vote, but only if they owned land. In 1869, the United Kingdom allowed women to vote in local (but not national) elections. The island of Corsica had full suffrage in 1755, but only until France took it over fourteen years later. Some states in Australia and the United States had full suffrage before 1893, but the whole countries took a while longer.

population, since New Zealand had always given Maori men voting rights and the same principle applied to Maori women.

Simply obtaining the right to vote didn't mean that women were actually able to vote; they still had to register in time for the election. Sheppard and the WCTU again started a national campaign, this time signing up as many voters as possible. The effort paid dividends, with about 65 percent of all eligible women casting a ballot in the first go. (Despite his opposition to voting rights, Seddon and his party retained power.)

———————

Sheppard continued her advocacy efforts once suffrage was won. In 1896, she was elected president of the New Zealand Council of Women and launched its magazine, which became the first Kiwi publication written and edited entirely by women. Though she moved back to Great Britain in 1903 and had plans to retire, she returned to New Zealand the following year because of severe health problems that required her to live in a warmer climate.

Despite decades of ill health, Kate Sheppard lived to age eighty-seven, dying on July 13, 1934. She outlived two husbands (widowed in 1915, she married again at seventy-eight), her only son, and even her only grandchild. She also lived long enough to see Elizabeth McCombs become New Zealand's first female MP in 1933. Sheppard remains one of the most important figures in New Zealand history; she is featured on the country's ten-dollar bill, and a statue depicting her along with fellow suffragettes stands in the city of Christchurch.

Though Sheppard's victory for voting rights received worldwide attention, other nations were slow to follow. It took nine years before Australia, in 1902, became the second country with women's suffrage, though it wasn't universal. (Aboriginal women were prevented from voting.) A few Scandinavian countries followed early in the twentieth century, and many more nations followed suit after World War I. ●

EMMA GOLDMAN

THE TIME: *1869–1940*

THE PLACES: *United States, Russia*

THE OPPONENTS: *Capitalism, war, gender inequality*

Pick a rebellious cause from the late 1800s or early 1900s, and odds are Emma Goldman took part in some way. A committed anarchist, she expanded her activism to include supporting the Russian Revolution, fighting for women's access to birth control, and organizing opposition to the military draft.

She was born in June 1869 in Lithuania, when it was still under the rule of the Russian czars, and grew up in a Jewish ghetto (though Orthodox by birth, she became a fervent atheist). The family later moved to Prussia and then to Russia, where, though her abusive father tried to prevent her from getting an education, Goldman studied on her own and took an interest in radical politics in her teen years.

In 1885, sixteen-year-old Emma Goldman moved from St. Petersburg to upstate New York, to join a sister who had already immigrated. There, she worked as a seamstress and became involved in the growing labor movement. She credited the following year's Haymarket strike and riot in Chicago with driving her to become an activist. The Haymarket strikers included a faction of anarchists, and Goldman was drawn to their anti-authority philosophy.

Moving to New York City in 1889 and taking a job in a clothing factory, she met the famous anarchist writer and publisher Johann Most, who took her under his wing and helped her develop her formidable public-speaking skills. In New York, she also met Alexander Berkman, who would become her partner in both romance and dissent for most of her life (she already had a brief, failed marriage while living in Rochester). New York had an active anarchist scene, and Goldman became part of it as a writer and speaker, advocating an end to capitalism and other forms of state power. In her writings, she described her version of anarchism as "the philosophy of the sovereignty of the individual" and "the theory of social harmony."

Goldman and Berkman put one controversial theory into practice during the 1892 Homestead Strike, a strike by Pennsylvania steel workers that was met with violent opposition. The factory manager, Henry Clay Frick, hired strike-breakers and private security guards to assault the strikers, killing several in the process.

Though the anarchist movement generally supported pacifism when it came to war, Johann Most preached what he called "propaganda of the deed"—the use of carefully targeted acts of violence to inspire uprisings. Under that premise, Goldman and Berkman plotted to assassinate Frick. On July 23, Berkman broke into Frick's office, shooting and stabbing (but failing to kill) the manager before being subdued.

Berkman was arrested, convicted of attempted murder, and sent to prison for the next fourteen years. Police figured Goldman had collaborated in planning the crime; they raided her apartment but couldn't find enough evidence to charge her. They did, however, convince her landlord to kick her out, and she was placed under frequent government surveillance.

Goldman continued to speak out for anarchist causes, and soon had her own run-in with the law.

In 1893, the American economy suffered its worst depression up to that point, causing massive unemployment. Goldman gave stirring speeches to thousands of unemployed workers, which scared authorities. After one particularly inflammatory speech in New York City's Union Square, she was arrested and charged with inciting a riot. She served ten months of a one-year sentence, but the publicity surrounding her arrest—and the well-publicized fact that she'd turned down a chance to avoid prison by informing on other anarchists—made her even more of a hero to her cause.

Goldman's higher profile caused its own problems. When an anarchist named Leon Czolgosz assassinated President William McKinley in 1901, Goldman was arrested and charged with inciting the crime, based on the killer's assertion that her speeches had inspired him to action. Though Czolgosz was mentally ill and admitted that Goldman had no direct involvement, she was still arrested and spent about two weeks in jail, during which time she was interrogated. The case against Goldman was eventually dropped, but her reputation suffered—as did that of anarchism itself, with many in the radical movement shifting their political philosophies.

Emma Goldman is not interested in your nonsense.

After the fallout from the McKinley assassination, Goldman briefly withdrew from public life, but in 1906 she started a monthly radical magazine called *Mother Earth*. The magazine published leading writers like Leo Tolstoy and Eugene O'Neill, while giving Goldman a national platform. Berkman (a type-setter by trade) was released from prison that same year, and later became the magazine's editor while Goldman traveled the country as a speaker and activist.

Her speaking tours drew huge crowds, and Goldman spent about half of every year on the road—visiting dozens of cities and giving as many as 120 speeches in just six months. Naturally, she ran afoul of the law again, when she supported feminist pioneer Margaret Sanger's push for birth control and contraception, despite state laws against them. Like Sanger, Goldman was arrested for violating the anti-obscenity Comstock Laws, and in 1916 she spent a couple weeks in prison.

Goldman agreed with many in the anarchist movement that war was a classic case of unchecked state power. So, when the United States entered World War I in 1917, she vehemently opposed it. And when Congress passed that year's Selective Service Act—requiring all men between twenty-one and thirty to register for a military draft—she urged potential draftees not to comply. She even formed a group called the No Conscription League, which organized anti-draft rallies and sent out pamphlets opposing the war.

On June 15, 1917, the federal government passed the Espionage Act—still technically on the books today—which made it illegal to interfere with military recruitment. The same day the law went into effect, Goldman's offices were raided, and she and Berkman were placed under arrest. Despite a spirited defense on free-speech grounds, they received the maximum sentence allowed—two years in prison, fines of $10,000, and the possibility of deportation. Goldman wrote that it was a small price to pay for taking "an uncompromising stand for one's ideal."

BIRTH CONTROL PIONEER

Though Goldman was already active in supporting similar measures before she met Margaret Sanger, it was Sanger who coined the term "birth control" and became the leader of the movement for legal contraception.

Starting in 1914, Sanger published a monthly magazine advocating for birth control, and authorities charged her with obscenity (for writing about how babies were made, and how to ensure they weren't). In 1916, after returning from a stretch abroad to avoid prison, she opened the nation's first birth-control clinic. The operation lasted only a few days before it was shut down and Sanger was briefly sent to jail—but the ruling in her appeal cleared the way for doctors to prescribe contraception. In 1921, Sanger founded the American Birth Control League; She opened the first legal birth-control clinic in the United States two years later (her organization would eventually turn into today's Planned Parenthood). She also advocated for new contraceptive devices, including the first birth-control pills.

A year before her death in 1966, Sanger saw the Supreme Court rule in favor of her cause, as the 1965 *Griswold v. Connecticut* decision struck down anti-contraception laws as violating the constitutional right to marital privacy.

By the time Goldman was released from prison in 1919, the United States was in the middle of a "Red Scare," using the Bolshevik Revolution in Russia (which she had vocally supported) as a pretext to crack down on leftists at home (see page 165). Within a month of leaving prison, Goldman faced a deportation hearing under the Alien Expulsion Act. She made a strong case that the law didn't apply to her—the charges against her were based on updates to the law while she was incarcerated, and it was supposed to apply only to non-citizens. The government, however, argued that she lost her citizenship in 1908 when her ex-husband lost his, a dubious argument even at the time. Seeing how the deck was stacked against her, Goldman didn't appeal the ruling.

A REVIVAL MOVEMENT

Goldman became popular again in the 1970s, when the publishing industry and feminist movement both revived her memory. *Living My Life* was reissued, and a feminist press put together a tome of her writings called *Red Emma Speaks*. In 1980, the University of California, Berkeley, began the Emma Goldman Papers Project, working to assemble documents by and about her, and publishing collections of them.

On December 21, 1919, the government deported her (along with Berkman and another 247 anti-draft activists) on a ship to the Soviet Union, which was still in the midst of its post-revolution civil war. Though Goldman had been a strong supporter of the Russian Revolution, seeing it as a needed corrective to both monarchy and capitalism, she considered what she saw in the Soviet Union a perversion of the revolution. By 1921, she had soured on Russia, and moved with Berkman several times before settling in Germany.

After leaving Berkman behind and moving to Great Britain, Goldman agreed to a paper marriage to a Scottish anarchist in 1925 so she could stay there legally. Working as a writer and drama critic, she later moved to Canada, then France, and then Spain (where she wrote firsthand essays on the Spanish Civil War).

Emma Goldman did make one last trip to the United States. In 1934, after she published an autobiography titled *Living My Life*, she applied for a short stay in her adopted homeland so that she could go on a book tour. The government agreed, on the condition that she only discuss the book (and the FBI still kept close tabs on her the whole time). Her visa only lasted three months, and she never returned again to the United States.

Goldman died in Toronto on May 14, 1940, at the age of seventy, after suffering two strokes within a month. Special permission from the United States government was required before her body could be returned for burial. Goldman is entombed in Waldheim Cemetery near Chicago, near the graves of the Haymarket activists who had first inspired her life of dissent. ●

MOHANDAS GANDHI

THE TIME: *1869–1948*

THE PLACE: *India*

THE OPPONENT: *Great Britain*

Mohandas Gandhi did not invent the concept of non-violence; after all, the idea simply involved not doing anything violent. But his strategy of using non-violent civil disobedience to mobilize large-scale movements was a radical idea—and a successful one. His peaceful activism for Indian civil rights and national independence made Gandhi one of history's most influential figures, still revered around the world, and a major inspiration for leaders like Martin Luther King, Jr., and Nelson Mandela.

Mohandas Karamchand Gandhi was born in 1869 in the western Indian state of Gujarat, where his father was a local politician. Men in the Gandhi family usually went into politics, and Mohandas's early career path reflected that. He graduated from law school in London and returned briefly to India in 1891, struggling to start a legal career.

The best offer he got was a one-year contract in South Africa. So, in 1893 he moved there to work as lawyer, and he ended up staying for two decades. He developed the philosophy and tactics he would use for the rest of his life while he was fighting discrimination in South Africa.

———

South Africa was decades away from legally creating apartheid, but the laws there were still deeply racist and society was segregated by race. Indian immigrants regularly faced discrimination, including in professions, like law, where they were perceived as competing with whites.

Some of Gandhi's personal experiences with South African racism have become legendary, especially a train trip he took from Durban to Pretoria. He was kicked out of a first-class cabin for refusing to give up his seat to a white passenger, and on a later leg of the same trip he was beaten by a white stagecoach driver when he didn't agree to ride outside the carriage so a white passenger could take his seat.

A stylish (but still quietly intimidating) Mohandas Gandhi stands for a portrait in South Africa in 1895.

These kinds of experiences weren't unusual for Indians in South Africa, and Gandhi used them as inspiration for a new way of standing up to such discrimination. Gandhi called his philosophy of resistance *satyagraha*. Rather than passive resistance, satyagraha, which translates as "devotion to truth" or "insistence on truth," meant actively standing up to wrongs and refusing to take part in any system that advanced them—but doing so through exclusively peaceful means.

Gandhi had been mostly apolitical before, but now he began organizing the Indian community in Natal, South Africa, and writing to government officials on its behalf. The trained lawyer sent well-argued grievances about how Indian immigrants—who were subjects of the British Empire, just like the South Africans—were deserving of the same rights.

His efforts put the subject into the public debate in Great Britain and abroad, making Gandhi an important and recognizable figure in the process. So much so that he was attacked and nearly killed by a white mob in 1897; in keeping with his philosophy, he did not press charges afterward.

In 1906, Gandhi organized his first major protest, one that would last nearly eight years. The government passed a law requiring all Indians in South Africa to register. At a protest in Johannesburg, he urged Indians not to comply with the law and to face whatever punishment the government would inflict. The punishments included prison—Gandhi personally went several times—as well as beatings and mob violence. Eventually, the negative publicity forced the government to negotiate with Gandhi to end the protests (though most racial discrimination remained).

In 1914, at age forty-five, Gandhi returned to India, where he took only a few years to become the leader of the Indian home-rule movement. Soon, it grew

PEACE TOWARD ALL

As part of his resistance to all forms of violence, Gandhi resisted violence against other species, becoming a vegetarian at a young age. As a law student, he joined the leadership of the London Vegetarian Society and met other activists through the vegetarian scene.

Gandhi saw vegetarianism as a key part of his overall philosophy, and in his book *The Moral Basis of Vegetarianism*, he argued that humankind's spiritual progress would ultimately result in an end of meat eating. One of Gandhi's most enduring quotes addressed this very issue: "The greatness of a nation and its moral progress can be judged by the way its animals are treated."

into a full-scale independence movement.

He first undertook smaller-scale activism against the British Raj government in India, like organizing indigo farmers in Bihar and poor farmers in Gujarat in protests against unfair taxation by the British Indian government. In both cases, he got the government to negotiate fairer terms.

In 1919, the government of India passed the Rowlatt Acts, which allowed it to arrest and imprison, without a fair trial, anyone suspected of sedition. During a Gandhi-organized anti-Rowlatt protest in Punjab, government troops fired on a group of about 10,000 peaceful protesters, killing at least 370 (and probably more). Though this "Amritsar Massacre" was obviously a blow to the home-rule movement, in the long run it convinced many Indians that the British-backed government had gone too far and had to be replaced.

Though Hindu himself, Gandhi was extremely popular among both Hindus and Muslims—the latter because he'd supported Muslim protests against Britain's treatment of the Ottoman Empire after World War I. With such broad support, by 1920 he became the most powerful figure in the Indian National Congress political party, and led the party's efforts toward independence.

Now with official as well as moral authority, he organized a massive non-cooperation protest, urging Indians to boycott certain British goods and institutions. For example, he encouraged all Indians to spin their own cloth to replace British imports, and did so himself. Though Gandhi tried to keep the movement peaceful, some clashes did break out between non-cooperation supporters and the government, and he had to cancel several planned actions.

That didn't stop the government from arresting Gandhi in March 1922 and imprisoning him on sedition charges, though he was released only two years into a six-year sentence. He tried to retire from politics at that point, but divisions in the INC meant the one man who could unite them had to return after a few years.

By 1930, he was back, leading a satyagraha protest. Gandhi brought more than 1,000 supporters on a monthlong "Salt March," which covered more than 200 miles. He was protesting a British law that prevented Indians from producing salt themselves, instead forcing them to buy imported salt with expensive taxes. The march ended on April 6, with Gandhi and his supporters collecting salt from the shore of the Arabian Sea—technically violating the law. The British again responded with mass punishment, jailing tens of thousands of people. But the government was starting to understand that it had to take the independence movement seriously.

―――――――――

Gandhi traveled to London in 1931, invited as the INC's representative to a British conference on the future of colonialism in India. Despite that sign of respect, the government had him arrested yet again on his return to India, after which he shifted his focus to internal matters—particularly improving the status of India's poorest caste, the "untouchables." Gandhi's tactics involved a long hunger strike, and his protests inspired reforms. He also continued working to foster good relations between Indian Muslims and Hindus, improve education for all Indians, and further develop his philosophy of non-violence.

He tried to retire from politics again in 1934, but it didn't last long—this time because of World War II. The INC put Gandhi back in charge, and he tried to get Britain to promise full withdrawal from India in exchange for its support during the war. Not surprisingly, Britain refused, instead having the entire INC leadership arrested and imprisoned in August 1942—and Gandhi spent *another* two years in prison.

After the war, however, Great Britain began to take apart what was left of its colonial empire, and the Indian independence Gandhi had sought for decades was finally a real possibility.

In June 1947, the newly elected Labour government agreed to Indian independence, but split the colony along religious lines into the modern states of India and Pakistan. Millions of people crossed the borders in both directions, and violence broke out during the transition, with up to half a million Indians and Pakistanis killed in riots. Gandhi opposed the split (and obviously the fighting) and protested with another prolonged fast.

Just a few days after he broke his fast, on January 30, 1948, Hindu extremist Nathuram Godse shot Gandhi as the seventy-eight-year-old made his way to prayers in New Delhi, violently killing the world's leading voice for nonviolence. Millions attended his funeral procession, and Gandhi remains one of the world's most beloved figures—almost always called Mahatma, an honorary name meaning "great soul" —and the recognized father of the Indian nation. ●

"Not John Lennon! V. I. Lenin!!
Vladimir Ilyich Ulyanov!!!"

VLADIMIR LENIN

THE TIME: *1870–1924*

THE PLACE: *Russia*

THE OPPONENT: *Russian aristocracy*

Before Vladimir Lenin led the Bolshevik Revolution of 1917, no country had ever tried implementing Communism on a large scale. By replacing the Russian aristocracy with the Communist Soviet Union, Lenin began one of the twentieth century's biggest experiments in government, one that would lead to both real and ideological warfare around the world and rank as arguably the most important revolution of its time.

Vladimir Ilych Ulyanov was born in the Russian town of Simbirsk on April 20, 1870. Though his father had worked his way up from modest means to a noble title and a job overseeing hundreds of schools, the Ulyanov family harbored an anti-authoritarian streak; all six children became revolutionaries to one degree or another.

Vladimir's older brother, Sacha, a university student at the time, joined a plot to assassinate Czar Alexander III in the spring of 1887. The plot was discovered, and Sacha was executed in May. Vladimir's own college experience ended after one term, when the school kicked him out for taking part in protests and the government placed him under surveillance.

The expulsion only made Vladimir a more committed revolutionary. Now in charge of his own education, he spent years reading revolutionary literature, including the writing of Karl Marx—the German political philosopher who foresaw a system in which the working class would take power, own the means of production together, and make Communism the ultimate step in society's evolution. Vladimir—by this point a self-described Marxist—finished his law degree remotely, and moved a few times, eventually to the capital of St. Petersburg. Along the way, he joined Marxist organizations and networked with other important revolutionaries.

The Russian regime understood the threat Marxism represented to its power, so it spied on and cracked down on Communist demonstrations and meetings. In 1895, Vladimir Ulyanov was arrested and exiled to Siberia, along with some of his revolutionary colleagues. He adopted the name Lenin shortly after serving his three-year exile in Siberia, and returned to Russia more committed than ever to Communist revolution.

Marxism included the idea of a worldwide workers' revolution, unbound by traditional nation-states. After his exile, Lenin spent much of his time trying to drum up support among revolutionaries in Western Europe, with stretches organizing Russian-born Communists in Switzerland, Great Britain, and Germany. He started a Communist newspaper (called *Iskra*) and in 1903 finalized the creation of a Marxist Russian political party (then called the Russian Social Democratic Labour Party).

The party had two main factions, and Lenin's loyalists took the name Bolsheviks (from the Russian word for "majority") to signal that they had more members than the more moderate Mensheviks. Though both factions (and others) took part in regular party conferences, Lenin and the Bolsheviks split off in 1912 and became an entity separate from the other Russian Marxist party.

While Russian Communists were busy organizing, the rest of Russian society was also turning against Czar Nicholas II and against the very idea of a sole ruler. The Russo-Japanese War, which started in 1904, proved a political and military disaster, cost Russia much of its navy and spawned a protest movement. In January 1905, a large crowd marched to the czar's palace to present a reform petition. Nicholas's security troops fired on the crowd, killing or wounding hundreds in an event appropriately called Bloody Sunday. A revolution of strikes and protests exploded around the country before the czar gave in and promised reforms, including the creation of an elected legislature (called the Duma).

By 1917, Russian anger at the czarist system had only increased, with Russia's 1914 entry into World War I (then known as the Great War) the last straw. Germany's vastly superior military was carving up Russian forces, as Russia suffered more casualties than any country in any modern war up to that point. The war was crushing Russia financially, food was scarce in the cities, and Nicholas had made few friends by executing political opponents, overseeing anti-Semitic violence, and repressing peaceful protests. Though he had allowed the Duma to exist, he also dissolved it again and again when it didn't vote how he wanted, making it mostly symbolic and effectively useless.

Many Russians had had enough, and even moderate voices came around to agree with what the Marxists already believed—that the czar had to go.

A WELL-PRESERVED REVOLUTIONARY

After his death, Lenin's body was embalmed and placed on display in a custom-built mausoleum in Moscow's Red Square. He's still on display there, in a clear coffin, with his body periodically preserved as needed (originally by the Soviet government, then with the aid of private donations after the USSR collapsed). Over the years, millions have seen his suit-wearing corpse, which remained in place except for a four-year stretch during World War II, when it was spirited out of Moscow and kept in Siberia while the capital was under Nazi occupation.

Lenin was in Switzerland when the Russian Revolution (confusingly called the February Revolution, because Russia still used the Julian calendar) overthrew the czar in March 1917. On March 8, tens of thousands of protesters marched on the capital, many more went on strike, and within a few days even the army had joined the call for a new government. Nicholas II was forced to abdicate and was placed under house arrest with his family, while a mix of moderate and liberal political parties began forming a provisional government.

Getting rid of the czar was a seismic event in Russia, but it also created a power vacuum. Although the German government was no fan of Lenin or his Bolshevik ideas, it did understand his potential ability to get Russia out of World War I. The year before, Lenin had written an influential book arguing against the war (blaming it on capitalism and imperialism) and openly hoping for Russia to lose the war as a step toward revolution.

Now that the czar was out of power, German officials helped Lenin and some supporters get back home—smuggled in a concealed train car—where Lenin began organizing the Bolshevik opposition to what he considered a not-radical-enough provisional government. The liberal government outlawed his party, and Lenin had to spend a short time in exile in Finland, plotting its overthrow.

He succeeded with the October Revolution of 1917 (in early November, again because of the calendar), when Bolshevik protesters took over the Winter Palace in St. Petersburg and captured the capital relatively peacefully. Before 1917 was over, Lenin began pulling Russia out of the war and setting up a government system controlled by a congress of workers' organizations called Soviets, from which the Soviet Union later took its name.

Though the October Revolution was largely bloodless, the civil war it prompted was anything but.

Within days of the Bolsheviks taking power, a loose coalition of anti-Communist forces—which included members of the czar's military, political opponents, and citizens of ethnic regions planning to form new states—began preparing for war, and these "White Russians" would face off against Lenin's "Red Russians." The war lasted until late in 1922, with more than 400,000 Russian soldiers killed in battle or from disease; the number of civilians killed was even greater.

Lenin and the Bolsheviks responded to the civil war harshly, establishing a secret police force (the *Cheka*). In July 1918, the deposed czar and his family were killed, ending the royal bloodline. The following month—after Lenin survived an assassination attempt that left a bullet in his neck—the government began what became known as the "Red Terror," the systematic execution of Russians considered "counterrevolutionaries." The measures worked to a point, as the Red Army ultimately won the civil war and Lenin remained in power, but the terror they inspired ended any chance of Russia becoming the egalitarian workers' paradise Lenin had claimed it would.

After the civil war, Lenin took on dictator-like powers, until a stroke in May 1922 left him unable to perform at full capacity. After recovering, he dictated his *Testament*, his proposal for fixing the Soviet Union and turning it into the Marxist state he envisioned. He had little time to implement those plans. Lenin suffered two more strokes—one in December 1922, which paralyzed his right side, and another three months later. That final stroke left him bedridden and unable to speak for the rest of his life, which ended January 21, 1924, at age fifty-three.

Lenin made it clear in his *Testament* that he feared power going to Joseph Stalin, and suggested Stalin's removal from office. His fears proved correct. Stalin took complete power after Lenin's death, purging the party by killing or exiling most of the Bolsheviks, rewriting Lenin's works to give himself a prominent role in the revolution (and creatively editing Lenin's appraisals of Stalin), and turning the USSR into a far more brutal dictatorship, one he would rule until 1953. ●

PANCHO VILLA

THE TIME: *1878–1923*

THE PLACE: *Mexico*

THE OPPONENT: *Several Mexican governments*

etween 1860 and 1920, the leadership of Mexico changed again and again, with a mix of foreign invasions, coups, revolutions, and betrayals installing a series of presidents. Pancho Villa never held the top job himself, but his career took him from being a bandit on the run from the law to becoming a key player in several changes of power, and a legendary revolutionary.

The name Pancho Villa was a pseudonym, adopted by Jose Doroteo Arango Arambula during his years as a bandit. Much of what's known about his early life might be simply legend. He was born June 5, 1878, in Durango, Mexico, the son of a poor sharecropper. Though some historians dispute this story, he claimed that at sixteen he shot and killed a man who raped his sister, then stole a horse and fled to the mountains to live as an outlaw bandit. No matter how it happened, at some point he joined one of the country's most notorious bandit gangs, and later became leader of his own band of outlaws.

Doroteo changed his name a few times during his years as a *bandolero* (the Spanish name for "bandit"). For a time, he was known as Arango, until he was arrested for stealing mules. He only avoided a death sentence by joining the army, but then deserted and went back to his outlaw life under the new name Francisco "Pancho" Villa. He and his followers stole horses, robbed banks, and hijacked shipments of goods, sometimes providing supplies to peasants in the area.

As a peasant outlaw who robbed from the rich, Villa became a kind of Robin Hood figure, known for his daring lifestyle and eventually for his support for the democratic cause. He was an early supporter of Francisco Madero, who in 1910 began a revolution to overthrow Mexican leader Porfirio Diaz and understood that the famous bandit's guerrilla tactics could come in handy.

Villa, riding high in the saddle.

Diaz, who had ruled the country as a dictator since an 1876 coup, had actually started out as a popular revolutionary. He made his name during the French Intervention, when France installed Maximilian I as emperor of Mexico in 1864. Diaz had been among the commanders who helped recapture Mexico City, after which the emperor was arrested and executed, and Benito Juárez was reinstalled as president. But a few years after Juárez died, Diaz seized power and ruled for more than thirty years.

Though Diaz had grown Mexico's economy significantly, that growth mostly benefitted wealthy citizens and foreign investors, widening the gap between the rich and the peasant class. Those conditions led to mass protests, including a push for a democratic Mexico. The revolution began after Diaz finally promised to hold an election in 1910, but once it became clear that his opponent, Francisco Madero, would defeat him in a vote, he instead threw Madero in prison and rigged the election.

Villa was among a number of fighters (including Emiliano Zapata and Casulo Herrera) who led revolts in support of Madero. He based his uprising in the northern Chihuahua region of the country and won a crucial battle at Ciudad Juárez. Though Madero had urged Villa not to attack the city—he was already negotiating with Diaz's government—Villa cut off all exits from Ciudad Juárez and took the city in close-quarters combat, rotating his soldiers in shifts to keep them fresh. Villa's victory, combined with Zapata's victory at Cuautla in the south, gave Diaz no choice but to agree to the rebels' terms.

The revolution prevailed in 1911, as Diaz resigned and Madero became president, naming Villa a colonel in the national army. Villa resigned his command soon after, partly so he could lead a quiet life with his new wife, and partly over differences with another of the former rebel commanders, Pascual Orozco. In the spring of 1912, however, Villa was back in action on Madero's side, fighting an attempted coup by Orozco. To make matters worse, General Victoriano Huerta—whom Villa had been fighting alongside in support of Madero—

accused him (probably falsely) of stealing a horse, and had Villa arrested and sentenced to death. The president commuted his sentence, but Villa still had to serve more than six months in jail before he escaped in December.

In the six months Villa had been locked up, the Mexican political landscape had changed dramatically.

Madero had proven to be a genuine democratic reformer, but he was more than a bit naive about political power and was betrayed by Villa's nemesis, Huerta. The general plotted to overthrow Madero, had him arrested, and executed him without trial four days later. Villa again joined forces with Zapata and Venustiano Carranza, this time to oppose Huerta. Villa controlled most of the north, and started to become a popular figure across the border in the United States, thanks to his impressive raids and his charismatic personality.

By 1914, the revolution had deposed Huerta, and Carranza had taken over as president. Villa became the governor of Chihuahua, elected by the military commanders of the area. Soon after, however, he and Carranza had a falling-out. Villa (and Zapata in the south) saw Carranza as another dictator when he refused to adopt the reforms he had initially promised. So, they continued their revolution, now against their former ally. Villa didn't fare as well in that round of fighting, losing three crucial battles in the spring and summer of 1915—the Battle of Celaya, the Battle of Trinidad, and finally the Battle of Agua Prieta. Those losses cost him most of his men, and he had to retreat to the mountains with about 200 remaining troops.

While he regrouped, Villa appealed to the United States for money and supplies, but received none. The United States had backed Villa and Carranza when they were on the same side, but wanted stability in Mexico and chose to recognize Carranza's government. Villa felt betrayed, and in January 1916 protested by executing a group of American citizens living in northern Mexico. He then turned his attention to the southwestern United States, carrying out the first

LIGHTS, CAMERA, ACTION!

Though film was still a relatively new medium during Villa's lifetime—the first, very basic movies came out in the 1890s—Villa understood the value of controlling his image. In 1913, he made a deal with Hollywood's Mutual Film Company, giving it exclusive rights to film his exploits and providing him a percentage of profits on any resulting films. The company's role in Villa's activities is often overstated, but it did film him in battle a number of times. In 2003, Antonio Banderas starred in *And Starring Pancho Villa as Himself*, a fictionalized movie about the 1913 movie deal.

Rival factions in Mexico not only competed with weapons, but also through song. "La Cucaracha," one of Mexico's quintessential *corrido* folk songs, predated the revolution (it might have even originated in Spain) but its lyrics were rewritten by supporters of several revolutionaries. The cockroach of the title, and what happens to it, changed depending on whether the singer saw Huerta or Villa as the bug in need of mocking. For what it's worth, the pro-Villa verses remain the most popular.

foreign attack on American soil since the War of 1812. He led a few hundred guerrillas against the town of Columbus, New Mexico. His men killed another group of Americans there, and President Woodrow Wilson responded by sending Brigadier General John Pershing to Mexico to retaliate.

Pershing had about 10,000 men at his command—and for the first time in American military history, airplanes—all of whom were tasked with hunting down Pancho Villa. Though they killed nearly 200 of his men, including some of his top commanders, they never got their hands on Villa himself. The Mexican public supported Villa, and his combination of guerrilla and bandit skills made him a hard man to catch. When Pershing and his men withdrew, in order to join the American forces fighting World War I, Villa's legend only grew.

Power changed hands yet again on May 20, 1920, when members of the Mexican army had Carranza assassinated. Adolfo de la Huerta claimed the presidency, and desperately wanted to end the constant warfare and turnover in the Mexican government. He offered Villa a chance to retire, and Villa agreed to stop fighting if the price was right. The new president obliged, pardoning him for all crimes and giving him a large hacienda at Parral in Chihuahua, where he and his remaining fighters could live in peace.

That peace didn't last. Villa was assassinated in 1923, while driving back to Parral after a trip to the bank. Seven riflemen—most likely working for his political rivals—ambushed his car and opened fire, killing Villa instantly. ●

MUSTAFA KEMAL ATATURK

THE TIME: *c. 1881–1938*

THE PLACE: *Turkey*

THE OPPONENT: *Ottoman Empire*

I t was inevitable that the Ottoman Empire was going to collapse in the early twentieth century, but that its largest state became a mostly democratic, secular, and modern Turkey was largely the revolutionary work of Mustafa Kemal Ataturk—a man whose Parliament-bestowed last name literally means "father of the Turks."

Then called only Mustafa, he was born in what was then called Salonika (now Thessaloniki, Greece), around 1881. At the time, the Ottoman Empire—which had existed since the late 1200s—was already in steep decline. Mustafa was an exceptional student; his second name of Kemal ("Perfect One") was given to him by an impressed teacher. He later enrolled at the War College in Constantinople and then graduated in 1905 with the rank of captain in the Ottoman army.

While still a student, Kemal began to protest the rule of the Ottoman sultan, Abdulhamid II—a notoriously autocratic ruler who dissolved Parliament, suspended the empire's 1876 constitution, and used a secret police force to crack down on dissent. In college, Kemal was caught working on an underground newspaper, but still graduated. Afterward, when he and some friends met in secret to discuss the sultan's policies, the government spied on them and then punished the "disloyal" young officers by making them serve far from the capital. In Kemal's case, that meant in Damascus, where he started a secret opposition group.

He was a supporter of the Young Turk Revolution, which began in July 1908 with an army division marching on the capital to demand the sultan reinstate

FRIENDLY ENEMIES

In a sign of the international respect he gained, there is even a Kemal Ataturk Memorial in Canberra, Australia, dedicated on the seventieth anniversary of the Gallipoli landing—even though he was leading the *other* side during that landing, commanding Turkish forces that thoroughly defeated the Australia/New Zealand Army Corps in a disastrous campaign. That owes partly to his chivalry in battle and partly to his respectful words about the Aussie/Kiwi forces he defeated—words now inscribed on that memorial in the Australian capital.

the constitution and Parliament. The Young Turks included a wide variety of groups and individuals who opposed Abdulhamid—from college intellectuals to nationalist supporters to ethnic minority groups. And they did force Abdulhamid out as sultan, filling the role with his brother Mehmed V, while restoring Parliament. Though the many factions of the Young Turks worked together at first, they splintered into rival groups—and the internal battles only weakened the Ottoman Empire while it fought a series of wars.

Though Kemal would later become the country's most important politician, he played almost no part in the coup and countercoups at the top. Instead, he made his name as a military commander during that period. He distinguished himself in 1911 during the Italo-Turkish War by winning the Battle of Tobruk, but Italy won the war and gained much of modern Libya from the Ottomans. From 1912 to 1913, Kemal fought in the Balkan Wars, in which the Ottoman Empire lost most of its European territory to a combined alliance of Greece, Bulgaria, Serbia, and Montenegro.

When the now-smaller empire entered World War I in 1914—joining Germany, Bulgaria, and Austria-Hungary in the Central Powers—Kemal was placed in charge of the defense at Gallipoli. He successfully turned away French and British attempts to take the peninsula in a campaign that cost the Ottomans and the Allies more than 56,000 troops apiece. As in 1911, however, Kemal won in battle only to see the empire lose the war.

The Ottoman leadership agreed to an armistice with the Allies on October 30, 1918—and that was the beginning of the end for an empire that had lasted almost 600 years. France, Italy, Great Britain, and Greece each occupied parts of the empire, and they began carving it up during the peace talks to end the Great War.

For Mustafa Kemal, the breakup of the Ottoman Empire was also an opportunity for Turkey to become an independent nation, so he began secretly building a Turkish National Movement. On May 19, 1919, Mustafa Kemal and his supporters landed in the Anatolia region, where they began reaching out to other nationalists and organizing a headquarters.

The Turkish War of Independence not only pitted Kemal's fighters (with aid from Russia) against Allied forces—primarily Greece on the western front and Armenia on the eastern—but those of the central Ottoman government in Constantinople. In addition to organizing the armed resistance, Kemal organized the institutions of a future Turkish state during his rebellion—most notably the 1920 creation of the Grand National Assembly of Turkey, a revolutionary parliament based in Ankara.

The revolutionary government eventually became the real government, especially once Britain—knowing Kemal's forces were advancing on Constantinople—invited both the Turkish and Ottoman governments to peace talks. The GNA preempted the talks by voting to end the Ottoman sultanate, and the sultan went into exile rather than fight on.

On July 24, 1923, the Allies and the GNA agreed to the Treaty of Lausanne. The agreement ended the war, with the Allies recognizing the nation of Turkey within treaty-confirmed borders. In exchange, Turkey agreed to give up any claims to the other parts of the Ottoman Empire. (The treaty also set borders for independent Bulgaria and Greece, and determined which parts of the formerly Ottoman Middle East would fall under French or British control.)

Kemal's forces entered Constantinople on October 2, and on October 29 he declared an independent Turkish republic, with Ankara as its capital. To no one's surprise, Mustafa Kemal was elected Turkey's first president the same day, and he set about an ambitious reform program that affected nearly every aspect of Turkish life.

On the cultural side, Kemal focused on modernizing Turkey by aligning it with Western practices. He replaced the centuries-old use of Arabic writing with the Latin alphabet and emphasized the Turkish language by banning certain uses of Arabic. He switched the country to the Gregorian calendar used in

Ataturk in the midst of World War I.

Western Europe, and he even formally changed the name of Constantinople to its already-in-use replacement, Istanbul.

Under his leadership, the GNA passed a new 1924 constitution with a separation of powers and a representative legislature, chosen in free elections. In March 1924, Turkey forever changed the role of religion in the state by abolishing the Ottoman Caliphate, removing Sunni Islam's official position in governing the country and making the government officially secular. Two years later, Kemal replaced the Islamic court system with a new penal code.

His reforms also ended the gender segregation the caliphate had mandated. Within a few years, women in Turkey were able to vote and to stand for office. Religious schools were closed, and public officials were forbidden from wearing Islamic dress. Instead, he encouraged all Turks to adopt Western-style clothing, even banning the traditional fez hat.

Despite his military background, Kemal successfully kept Turkey out of war; the war of independence was the country's last campaign against another nation. Instead, he deployed effective diplomacy and even signed a 1930 peace treaty with Greece, improving the Turks' most historically fraught relationship. (Turkey did, however, fight a rebellion by the Kurds within its treaty-defined borders.)

Domestically, Kemal focused on building a new education system, with modern universities and a formalization of the Turkish language. He formed organizations to study and publish Turkish history, translate scientific information into Turkish, and encourage the study of Western-style arts and music. He organized a state-run economy at first, building institutions like a central bank and national railroad system.

In 1926, he had told his countrymen that "the civilized world is far ahead of us," but under his leadership, Turkey made up significant ground in only about a decade. Some of his reforms were unpopular, especially among the religious community; still, there was no question Kemal had made Turkey far more modern than the state it replaced.

Though he never had biological children (he did adopt several, including Sabiha Gökçen, who became the world's first female fighter pilot), the GNA officially renamed him the father of his country when giving him Ataturk as a last name in 1934.

In his last years, he struggled with cirrhosis of the liver, from which he died at fifty-seven, on November 10, 1938. He remains the most revered figure in Turkey, with a memorial in every city and a national moment of silence still held every year on the date and exact time of his death. •

MARCUS GARVEY

THE TIME: *1887–1940*

THE PLACE: *United States*

THE OPPONENT: *Racial dynamics*

By the early twentieth century, some members of the African-American civil rights movement were focused on ways to achieve full equality right away, while others focused on ways to gradually integrate the community into the existing American power structure. Marcus Garvey, however, felt that both approaches were wastes of time. Instead, he believed African-Americans should separate from the rest of the country and re-establish themselves simply as Africans—and he began a millions-strong political movement around that idea.

Garvey was born in Jamaica, in August 1887. Though he left school at fourteen to take a job as an apprentice printer, politics soon emerged as his true passion. At first, he focused on the labor movement, with Garvey helping to lead a printers' strike in Kingston when he was twenty. He later traveled around Central America, reporting for newspapers about the conditions of migrant farm workers in Costa Rica and Panama.

While studying in London for two years, Garvey also wrote for the *African Times and Oriental Review*, a magazine for black and Asian readers that advocated pan-Africanism—a belief that people of African descent around the world were linked as a diaspora (people displaced from their true homeland) and should unite for common goals.

In 1914, when Garvey moved home to Jamaica, he put his support of pan-Africanism into action by forming the Universal Negro Improvement Association. He wanted UNIA to develop career and educational opportunities for black Jamaicans, using the model of the Tuskegee Institute—the Alabama school for African-Americans founded by Booker T. Washington. Garvey corresponded with Washington about his plans, and they discussed Garvey relocating to the

United States to raise money for his organization (though Washington died before Garvey arrived).

———————

Garvey made the move to the United States in 1916, arriving with little money and staying with various Jamaican families in New York City's Harlem neighborhood. The heavily African-American-populated area was just about to enter its "Harlem Renaissance" artistic heyday, drawing influential leaders and movements to the neighborhood, and was fertile ground for Garvey's message of black nationalism. In May 1917, Garvey started the first UNIA chapter in the United States, growing it from thirteen initial members to a few thousand in its first few months. By early 1918, he had used his printing background to launch a weekly pan-African paper, the *Negro World*. His appeals to the community often focused on the idea of black pride, and the notion of creating African-American-owned businesses and institutions. He also bought an auditorium in Harlem he renamed Liberty Hall, where the UNIA held nightly meetings and Garvey had a platform for his public pronouncements.

Economic independence was only one part of the philosophy that became known as "Garveyism." After observing racism in New York, Marcus Garvey drifted away from Washington's goal of assimilation, believing that full racial integration could never happen in America. He ultimately championed a full division between black and white society, wanting African-Americans to build a completely separate infrastructure of their own.

More controversially, he believed all members of the African diaspora should ultimately return to the African continent, and raised money for this "Back to Africa" movement. To turn his words into actions, Garvey in 1919

BACK TO AFRICA

Garvey's wasn't the first movement to advance the idea that black Americans should return to Africa. The country of Sierra Leone was founded in the late 1700s by Great Britain specifically as a place to resettle former slaves from the American colonies and the Caribbean. The first settlement (still the capital) was named Freetown, and Britain settled more freed slaves there after ending its slave trade in 1807. The neighboring nation of Liberia was created in 1820 by the American Colonization Society, a mostly abolitionist group committed to resettling freed slaves. Its capital was named Monrovia in honor of president (and colonization supporter) James Monroe, the flag was modeled on the United States flag, and Liberia became independent in 1847 with a constitution inspired by the United States Constitution.

founded the Black Star Line, a steamship company he planned to use to sell goods internationally and eventually transport potential expatriates to Africa. Within three months of forming the company, Garvey purchased a used coal ship (paying several times what it was worth), and staffed it with an all-black crew.

Garvey in 1924, taking a brief break from doing it all.

By 1920, Garvey claimed UNIA had grown to more than four million members (probably a high estimate of a legitimately large number). He started hosting annual "Garvey parades" in Harlem, where he would appear in a purple-and-yellow military uniform and feathered helmet, and lead tens of thousands of Harlem residents in marches. The parades included uniformed members of various clubs Garvey started, like the Universal African Legion, African Black Cross Nurses, and the Black Flying Eagle Corps of trained pilots. By that point, UNIA had expanded to hundreds of chapters around the world. In August 1920, Garvey hosted UNIA's first international convention at Madison Square Garden, speaking before a crowd of about 25,000 delegates.

While Garvey was acquiring supporters and influence, he was also making enemies. W. E. B. Du Bois—a pan-Africanist and co-founder of the NAACP—called Garvey "the most dangerous enemy of the Negro race in America and in the world" for his separatist views. Also, the Bureau of Investigation (which would become the FBI) had started keeping tabs on Garvey in 1919. Under the leadership of J. Edgar Hoover, the organization spent more than five years monitoring UNIA members in about two dozen chapters and coordinating similar efforts by other intelligence agencies. Hoover was quite open about wanting to

RELIGIOUS HONORS

Not only is Garvey a national hero (officially named as such by the government) in his home country of Jamaica, but the Rastafari religious movement there adopted him as a prophet. Though the movement wrote Garvey and his ideas into its folklore, he was not a Rastafari. Garvey identified as Catholic, and had been openly critical of Ethiopia's emperor, the man Rastafari supporters considered the Second Coming prophesied in the Bible.

Many African nations created more secular tributes to Marcus Garvey. The West African country of Ghana gave him some of the most creative ones, naming its national soccer team the Black Stars in Garvey's honor, calling its shipping line the Black Star Line, and placing a black star in the center of its flag as another tribute.

deport Garvey, but needed his quarry to commit a federal crime first.

In a remarkably tone-deaf example of politics making strange bedfellows, in 1922 Garvey met with Edward Clark, the leader of the white-supremacist Ku Klux Klan. The Klan (for different reasons than Garvey's, obviously) agreed with him about separating the races and supported sending African-Americans overseas. The meeting turned numerous former supporters against Garvey, and other civil rights groups began to criticize and mock him.

It was the Black Star Line, however, that ultimately gave Hoover a chance to act on his fear of Garvey. The shipping company had been a fiasco from the start, with UNIA overpaying for its ships, hiring employees who stole cargo, and losing more than $1 million—much of it raised from relatively poor investors who believed in Garvey's politics.

The mismanagement gave federal investigators a reason to go after the Black Star Line, and they zeroed in on a flier Garvey had mailed to supporters to raise funds for an additional ship. UNIA had included an image on the leaflet of a ship with the name Garvey had chosen for it—only the ship wasn't purchased yet, and the image wasn't of any specific craft the group was planning to buy. For the FBI, that was cause enough to arrest Garvey in 1922 and indict him on charges of mail fraud.

What the prosecution deemed fraud, Garvey's supporters saw as mere technicalities and sloppy bookkeeping, viewing the allegations against him as a political attack. Still, UNIA's records were indisputably wrong, and Garvey's decision to act as his own lawyer didn't do him any favors. The jury found him guilty on June 23, 1923, sentencing Garvey to five years in jail. Though President Calvin Coolidge commuted the last few years of Garvey's prison sentence in November 1927, it was only so the government could deport Garvey back to Jamaica.

Garvey returned to his homeland a popular figure, and was met by a large crowd when he landed in Kingston. Though he continued promoting pan-African ideals, he also became involved in politics at home, founding the People's Political Party, Jamaica's first modern political party. Its platform included an eight-hour workday and a standard minimum wage.

However, Garvey's second act in Jamaica also included some shadier scenes. He continued to correspond with white supremacists in America, working with the notoriously racist Senator Theodore Bilbo of Mississippi to try passing a law to relocate millions of black Americans to Africa (the bill failed), and promoting an anti-Semitic conspiracy theory about the motivations of the judge and prosecutor in his mail-fraud case. He also served time in a Jamaican jail for contempt of court against a local judge. In 1935, his reputation tarnished, he left Jamaica and moved to London.

Marcus Garvey wound up spending the rest of his life in Great Britain, dying on June 10, 1940. (There's a story, possibly apocryphal, that the stroke that killed him came when he read a premature obituary the *Chicago Defender* had published a few months earlier). In 1964, his remains were moved from London to Jamaica, where he was buried in the National Heroes Park. •

MICHAEL COLLINS

THE TIME: *1890–1922*

THE PLACE: *Ireland*

THE OPPONENT: *United Kingdom*

For most of modern history, the island of Ireland has found itself dominated by England. Its neighbor across the Irish Sea invaded way back in the twelfth century, and English or British authorities occupied Ireland for more than 700 years. By the time Michael Collins and his fellow revolutionaries came on the scene, Irish independence had been a long time coming—and it would still cost many, many lives.

Michael Collins was born in Cork County, Ireland, on October 16, 1890. Collins moved to London as a teenager, where he attended college and worked as a postal clerk. Though he was already a supporter of Irish republican goals—thanks to his schoolteacher and a local blacksmith who both inspired him—in London he joined the political party Sinn Fein (Gaelic for "we ourselves") as well as the Irish Republican Brotherhood, a secret society. Both organizations were committed to finally getting Ireland out from under British rule. By the time Collins moved back to Ireland in 1916, the pro-independence movement was only growing.

If not for World War I, Ireland would have probably had a fair amount of independence already. In the 1870s, a "home rule" movement had gained ground in Ireland, seeking an arrangement in which the country would have far more self-government while remaining within the United Kingdom. When the 1910 parliamentary election ended with the UK's two main parties holding equal strength, the Irish Parliamentary Party had the tie-breaking leverage it needed to make a deal—supporting the Liberal Party's finance bill in exchange for the Liberals supporting Irish home rule.

The House of Commons passed a Home Rule Act in 1914 . . . but its implementation was repeatedly delayed by the Great War. The government even passed a law requiring home rule to wait until the end of the war, and the war kept dragging on.

On Easter Monday 1916, republic supporters in Ireland made their displeasure heard—issuing a proclamation declaring Ireland a republic and organizing a show of force to back that position. In the middle of the day, about 1,200 rebels (including Michael Collins, who was not yet a major figure in the movement) took over key buildings throughout Dublin. Within a few hours, they captured most of their targets—most notably the General Post Office—and cut the phone lines to the British stronghold of Dublin Castle.

MOVIE TREATMENT

Renewed interest in the story of Michael Collins came with a 1996 biopic. Though a Hollywood film, it had a definite Irish character—it was written and directed by Neil Jordan, starred Liam Neeson in the title role (along with Stephen Rea and Irish-American Aidan Quinn), and featured Irish singers like Sinéad O'Connor and Frank Patterson on the sound track. Though it performed modestly in the United States, *Michael Collins* was briefly the top-grossing film of all time in Ireland (eventually supplanted by *Titanic*). The Irish government, considering the film an important work, even lowered its appropriate-age rating to encourage Irish teens to see it.

Two days later, however, the British army went after the rebels. Armed only with rifles and outnumbered about twenty to one, the republicans stood little chance. The army treated Irish civilians as if they were in league with the rebels, killing as many as 1,000 (though losing about 500 soldiers in the process) and destroying much of central Dublin. In just four days, the British army forced the leaders of the rebellion to surrender, publicly marching the arrested rebels through the streets. A military court tried and executed the rebellion's leaders in secret, only announcing the killings after the fact.

The cost had been high, but the heavy-handed British response to the Easter Uprising gave the rebels what they wanted. Before and during the uprising, the rebels had a hard time convincing the Irish public that Ireland should be independent (many people even came out to boo the ringleaders during their arrests). The crackdown, though, made the UK actually look as oppressive as the revolutionaries described it. Home rule within the UK was no longer a realistic goal after that Easter; it was full independence or bust.

Though Collins was arrested during the Easter Uprising, his profile was low enough for him to avoid the death penalty. He remained in prison in Britain until his release in December 1916, and the huge man nicknamed "The Big Fellow" returned to Ireland with a significantly bigger reputation. Collins won election to the executive committee of the republican political party Sinn Fein, and became a leading voice calling for Ireland to fight for a full break from British rule. In his view, the Irish would need to accomplish this through politics as well as through battle.

Sinn Fein dominated Ireland in the 1918 UK general election, sweeping all but the far north of the island and picking up seventy-three out of 105 total Irish seats. Michael Collins was elected a member of Parliament, representing the southern part of Cork, earning a seat in the United Kingdom House of Commons.

Collins during a St. Patrick's Day speech in 1922.

Rather than take their seats in London, however, Sinn Fein members announced a plan to instead start their own Irish Parliament (named Dáil Éireann) in Dublin. The British government wasn't going to let what it considered part of its territory start its own legislature. Collins was tipped off about a plan to arrest party members, and tried to warn the rest. Quite a few were caught in night raids, but Collins was among those who managed to avoid arrest.

The remaining members of the Irish Parliament followed through on their plan, convening in January 1919 and—on the Dáil's first day—declaring Ireland an independent republic, starting the Irish War of Independence. With so many republicans killed or imprisoned, Michael Collins became a leader fairly quickly. He was appointed minister of finance, and successfully raised the money the young government needed through selling bonds to supporters.

One of the Dáil's first objectives was to start its own military. What had been the Irish Volunteers became the far more organized Irish Republican Army (IRA), and Collins became its director of intelligence shortly after its creation.

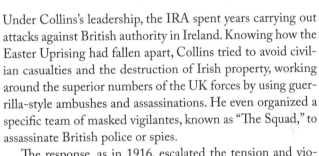

Under Collins's leadership, the IRA spent years carrying out attacks against British authority in Ireland. Knowing how the Easter Uprising had fallen apart, Collins tried to avoid civilian casualties and the destruction of Irish property, working around the superior numbers of the UK forces by using guerrilla-style ambushes and assassinations. He even organized a specific team of masked vigilantes, known as "The Squad," to assassinate British police or spies.

The response, as in 1916, escalated the tension and violence. The existing Royal Irish Constabulary (RIC)—the British police in Ireland—added two forces (the Auxiliary Division and the Black and Tans), made up mostly of World War I veterans. Those forces often acted more like paramilitaries than police, massacring civilians in response to the more targeted IRA actions. Less disciplined than the RIC, the Auxiliaries and Black and Tans burned and looted Irish homes, terrorizing the population. These tactics, however, only served to make civilians more likely to aid the IRA.

On the notorious Bloody Sunday—November 21, 1920—IRA gunmen killed fourteen British officers in one day in Dublin. The Black and Tans retaliated by attacking an in-progress football match at Croke Park in Dublin, driving

HISTORIC ANNIVERSARY

Every year on its anniversary, Ireland holds a commemoration of Collins's death at the spot where it took place. In 2012, the event itself made quite a bit of history. The armored Rolls-Royce (nicknamed Sliabh na mBan) that Collins was driving that day made an appearance, as did Enda Kenny—the first time an Irish head of government attended the ceremony. The country's bank also released limited-edition coins to commemorate the ninetieth anniversary of Collins's death. That same year, newly discovered IRA documents provided more detail regarding what happened on the day of the murder.

armored vehicles into the stadium and killing a dozen people, including one player. The war became bloodier after that point, with roughly 1,000 people killed just between December 1920 and July 1921—far more than in the first few years of the conflict combined.

By July 1921, the two sides could see the situation was unsustainable, and agreed to a truce. In October, Collins represented Ireland as the lead negotiator in peace talks with Great Britain. The result of three months of negotiations, the Anglo-Irish Treaty recognized Ireland as a free and self-governing nation within the British Commonwealth, with six pro-Union counties in the north (what's now Northern Ireland) remaining part of the UK. To Collins and the pro-Treaty faction, it was an important step toward independence. To some Irish hardliners, however, the deal was unacceptable because it stopped short of full independence for all of Ireland.

Though the treaty was passed quickly by the British government, the Dáil and the Irish cabinet were deeply divided. The agreement did eventually (but barely) pass, and Collins became chairman of a provisional government. But anti-Treaty forces split Sinn Fein into two parties and the IRA into rival armies that would soon fight each other in a ten-month Irish Civil War. It didn't end until anti-Treaty forces surrendered in May 1923.

Collins led the pro-Treaty IRA forces for a time, but didn't live to see the end of the Irish Civil War. After signing the treaty, he had reportedly said, "I have signed my death warrant," and events proved him right. His car was ambushed on August 19, 1922, near the small village of Béal na mBláth. Only thirty-one at the time, Collins was shot by unknown anti-Treaty IRA assassins. His funeral drew thousands of mourners, and the circumstances of his death have inspired conspiracy theories ever since. ●

HO CHI MINH

THE TIME: *c. 1890–1969*

THE PLACE: *Vietnam*

THE OPPONENTS: *France, Japan, United States*

Throughout his adult life, Ho Chi Minh had one goal: the creation of an independent Vietnamese state. And throughout his life, that goal meant he faced off against some of the world's most powerful nations, from France to Japan to the United States. His revolutionary ideas were a rare combination of anti-colonial nationalism and a Communism focused on pragmatism above ideology. Though he didn't live to see that result, and many died in the process, his efforts restored an independent Vietnam.

When Ho was born, in about 1890, France had recently turned much of Southeast Asia into the colony of French Indochina. As it did elsewhere, it introduced French education and language, while spreading Catholicism and instituting an economic system that turned local resources into commodities for France (without doing much for the locals). French rule would spark numerous protests and rebellions in Vietnam, though none had much success until Ho.

Before adopting the name Ho Chi Minh during his revolutionary leadership, he was called by his birth name Nguyen Sinh Con, and was later known as Nguyen Tat Thanh and Nguyen Ai Quoc. His father had served as an imperial magistrate and a teacher, but was also a stark opponent of French rule who refused to learn the language.

Still, Nguyen attended a Western-style school and worked briefly as a teacher before spending much of his twenties working on ships and traveling the world, living in France, the United States, and Great Britain.

He was living in France during the later part of World War I, and while there organized his first attempt to challenge French rule of his homeland. Nguyen put together a group of Vietnamese expats, who went to the 1919 Versailles Peace Conference and petitioned the delegates there to recognize the civil rights of French Indochina's citizens. He particularly hoped the United States delegation would back him, considering the country's own history of independence from a colonial power . . . but his petition got no support in Versailles, from the U.S. or any other nation.

The next year, he became a cofounder of the French Communist Party and joined its Colonial Committee, giving him a platform to speak out about the abuses of French colonialism in Indochina, and building on the anti-colonial bona fides he earned at Versailles. He moved around for much of the next two decades, attending a Communist university in the Soviet Union before serving as an organizer and advisor for Marxist movements in China and elsewhere in Asia. In 1930, he organized Vietnamese expats in a growing independence movement and founded the Indochinese Communist Party.

Unlike many key Communist leaders of the era, Ho was a nationalist first, seeing Communism as a way of liberating Vietnam rather than seeing the liberation of Vietnam as a way to advance Communism. Already past fifty, in 1941 he finally returned home to make that goal a reality.

———————

His first action in his home country involved fighting Japan, which had invaded Indochina while France was busy fighting Germany on the western front of World War II. He had adopted the name Ho Chi Minh (which roughly translates to "bringer of light") by that point and started an armed resistance movement he named the Viet Minh.

The Viet Minh, though many of its members were also Communists, was designed as a pro-independence army. And because it was fighting Japan, it received support from the United States, China, and the other Allies. The Viet Minh grew to include about half a million members, and put together a 10,000-

AN AMERICAN INSPIRATION

Ironically, considering the future involvement of the United States in Vietnam, Ho was an admirer of the American Revolution and based his 1945 constitution on the American one. He wasn't able to get a copy of it while writing, and used what he could remember from his time living in the United States. He got pretty close, with his constitution opening, "All men are created equal; they are endowed by their Creator with certain inalienable Rights; among these are Life, Liberty, and the pursuit of Happiness."

man guerrilla unit (the "Men in Black") that used jungle warfare and ambush tactics with great success against Japanese forces, who were much less familiar with the terrain.

When World War II ended in 1945, Japan withdrew and Ho declared an independent Vietnam with Hanoi as its capital. Then France came back into the picture.

Ho and his supporters had firm control in the north of the country, but France reclaimed the southern city of Saigon and began trying to take back more of its former colony. Ho tried negotiating a deal that would have made Vietnam a free state within the French sphere—which did get

Ho Chi Minh in a portrait from c. 1946.

China to withdraw its own postwar occupying force from the north—but the agreement failed, and the two sides went to war.

The Viet Minh would fight France and its anti-Communist Vietnamese allies for almost nine years. The deciding moment was the 1954 Battle of Dien Bien Phu, where French forces tried to cut off Viet Minh supply lines and force the Communist guerrillas into open battle. Which they did, but the Viet Minh had already surrounded the French position, giving the Vietnamese the high ground and a perfect position for attack using a lot more heavy artillery than the French forces expected.

The defeat convinced France to negotiate an end to its occupation, and the sides agreed to terms in July. The deal agreed to in those postwar Geneva Accords divided Vietnam at the 17th parallel, setting up a Communist Democratic Republic of Vietnam in the north (with Ho as president) and a state in South Vietnam with Western support.

Under the terms of the Geneva agreement, the two Vietnams were scheduled for a reconciliation vote in 1956. By that point, it was obvious to everyone that North Vietnam had the numbers to win any election, as the man commonly called "Uncle Ho" was an incredibly popular figure in most of the region. (American president Dwight Eisenhower predicted that Ho might get 80 percent support if a vote were held.) The president of South Vietnam, Ngo Dinh Diem, was anything but popular, and decided not to follow the Geneva deal. Communist guerrillas in South Vietnam, called the Viet Cong, began to carry out attacks against the government there once the election was canceled. North

NOT JUST IDEOLOGICAL PURITY

Both during and after his lifetime, Ho was such a revered figure in Vietnam that supporters turned him into a folk hero. Like those of Vladimir Lenin and Mao Zedong, his body is still displayed in a public mausoleum—even though Ho wanted to be cremated.

Part of his posthumous legend involves Ho devoting himself completely to the cause of forming a Vietnamese nation. So, the idea that he might have devoted himself to a woman for even a night became taboo, as if that meant cheating on the country. In 2002, the government banned a new book that discussed Ho's love life (including a brief marriage) and any media that discussed the controversy over the banned book. Because Ho left no biological heir, the party still teaches that he was celibate (at least once he became a revolutionary) and encourages party members to follow that example . . . which could become a problem for the future of party membership.

Vietnam backed them up and provided them with supplies while cracking down on suspected sympathizers, and the fighting expanded into a war.

Fearing another Communist state in Asia after Mao Zedong's revolution in China (see page 191), the United States backed the government of South Vietnam, first with aid, then with military advisors, and, by 1965, with deployments of combat troops. And so began the Vietnam War (or the Second Indochina War, as it was called on Ho's side), a gruesome conflict that matched overpowering American weaponry against harsh guerrilla fighting. Ho had given up day-to-day leadership of North Vietnam by the late 1950s, but he remained head of state in name and was still an important big-picture revolutionary as the conflict escalated.

Though Ho consistently (and correctly) predicted that Vietnam would outlast another occupying nation, he didn't personally outlast the conflict. After years of health problems, he died on September 2, 1969, at the age of seventy-nine. The war continued without him for years, until March 29, 1973, when President Richard Nixon withdrew the last American combat troops from Vietnam.

Two years later, the South Vietnamese capital of Saigon fell, removing the last major obstacle to a unified but Communist Vietnam. The war ultimately cost more than 58,000 American lives and probably at least 800,000 Vietnamese lives (some estimates go above one million). On July 2, 1976, after more than a year of northern military occupation of the south, the two Vietnamese states unified as the Socialist Republic of Vietnam, and Saigon was renamed Ho Chi Minh City. ●

MAO ZEDONG

THE TIME: *1893–1976*

THE PLACE: *China*

THE OPPONENT: *Republic of China*

For more than fifty years, first as a revolutionary against the government and then as head of a revolutionary government, Mao Zedong fought for and created a Communist China that would reflect his own ideas. Mao would ultimately kill millions of his own people in pursuit of his people's republic, but the state he created has lasted more than sixty years.

The son of a peasant farmer, Mao Zedong (also called Mao Tse-tung) was born in Hunan Province in 1893. In 1911, the Qing dynasty, which had ruled China since 1644, collapsed and was replaced by the country's first republic. Mao served a short stint in Sun Yat-Sen's revolutionary army during the last six months before the dynasty fell and then resigned to try a sampling of academic pursuits, switching his planned career several times. While working at a university library, he was inspired by the success of the Communist revolution in Russia (see page 165) and became involved in student protests.

In 1921, Marxists around the country founded the Chinese Communist Party, with Mao starting one of the chapters. That same year, Sun—who had served as president only briefly after his earlier revolution—set up a military government in Guangzhou. In the years after the Qing dynasty fell, China was run by a series of regional governments—including powerful warlords in the north—and Sun was set on unifying the country.

Sun actually accepted the Communists' help as they teamed up with his Kuomintang (KMT) party to fight the various warlords, while opposing both the national government and foreign influence in China (except for that of Soviet Russia, which provided aid for the cause).

The revolution could have ended there, but Sun died in 1925. And the man who replaced him, Chiang Kai-shek, turned on the Communists. At first, he just kicked them out of leadership positions. In 1927, however, Chiang started killing and arresting Communists, including the killing of a few thousand in Shanghai. Mao led a peasant revolt against him, but his effort failed, and Mao fled with some supporters to the southeast of China. Less than halfway through 1927, the CCP had lost up to 60 percent of its members in the purge.

Mao had been a fairly minor player before the purge, but soon became a major one, setting up a base in Jiangxi Province and building a guerrilla army. He declared the area the Soviet Republic of China (with himself as its head) and began a long revolution that would last more than two decades, with his CCP fighting Chiang's KMT.

The achievement that clinched Mao as an effective leader was the 1934 "Long March." Tipped off that Chiang and a force of about one million government troops were planning an attack, Mao convinced the other Communists that retreat was the best plan and led about 100,000 supporters on an organized escape to the country's northwest. Though fewer than half the Communists survived the 8,000-mile retreat, the survivors' success at escaping Chiang's forces became a rallying—and a recruiting—point in their favor.

The revolution went on an eight-year hiatus when China was drawn into full-scale war with Japan. In 1937, the Japanese—who had already invaded and captured the Chinese province of Manchuria in 1931—invaded the heart of China. So, as they had during the conflict with the warlords, the KMT and CCP joined forces to fight a common enemy, putting their differences aside until the end of World War II.

Mao looks ahead in this 1931 photograph.

Almost as soon as the Allies defeated Japan, the civil war in China started right back up. Mao and other CCP leaders had learned effective tactics while fighting Japan and used these strategies against Chiang's larger army.

To spread his political views, Mao published in 1966 *Quotations from Chairman Mao*, now commonly referred to as the *Little Red Book*. He published other books, too, with words spoken by Mao always printed in red so they would stand out from the rest of the text. The *Little Red Book* was mandatory—party members were expected to carry it with them, and an edition was printed small enough for soldiers to keep in their pockets at all times. As a required book in a country with a population above one billion, the *Little Red Book* has become the second-most-printed book of all time, trailing only the Bible.

In Beijing's Tiananmen Square, on October 1, 1949, Mao declared the People's Republic of China, also declaring himself its chairman. Chiang and other refugees from his government fled for the island of Taiwan, where they would set up a new Republic of China, which remains independent to this day (though few countries have recognized its sovereignty).

On the mainland, Mao and the CCP began to create a new form of Chinese Communism. He put both industry and agriculture under state control, including a program of turning private farms into collectives. Mao's goal was to quickly grow an economy that lagged behind the world's other powers, and at first he requested input from Chinese citizens. Of course, Mao did not like all of their input, and in a preview of how his government would handle dissent, he had opponents killed or sent to work camps for what Mao called "re-education through labor."

While his revolution had managed to unite China, Mao's time as chairman is best remembered for two policies that tore it apart—the Great Leap Forward and the Cultural Revolution.

The teachings of Karl Marx had predicted Communism as the next stage for industrial countries, rather than agricultural ones. Mao's goal for the 1958 Great Leap Forward was to modernize agriculture and industry through a radical program of reorganizing the country into communes.

The effort failed spectacularly. Key resources were diverted from agriculture to industry, so that poor growing weather had more of an impact than usual. The huge decrease in food production led to a prolonged famine, with between 20 million and 40 million Chinese citizens dying of starvation or malnutrition in just a few years. Even Mao admitted the program was a disaster, and he gave up his title as head of state (but, as chairman, he was still a powerful man in China).

While the agricultural program killed millions through poor planning, the Cultural Revolution killed millions more as part of the plan.

DOING THE MATH

In the years after Mao's death, the Chinese government had to struggle with how to treat his legacy. His cult of personality meant many of Mao's supporters saw him as perfect, and the state had taught that this was the correct view.

The new president, Deng Xiaoping, had a creative solution.

In 1981, his government declared that Chairman Mao's actions and ideas had been 70 percent right and 30 percent wrong. The math behind those percentages wasn't terribly clear, and the government didn't go into great detail about which ideas fit which category. (An open public debate about where Mao went wrong still hasn't happened in China.) The declaration did, however, give Deng the political cover to break with Mao's precedents as needed and institute reforms without the government officially overturning or invalidating Mao's legacy.

Starting in 1966, Mao reasserted his authority and attempted to purge anyone he perceived as a critic of his goals for the party. He claimed that certain elements in the country were trying to bring back capitalism and ordered witch hunts against anyone suspected of disloyalty. His People's Liberation Army was joined by groups of students called Red Guards, who spied on, exiled, and executed Mao's political opponents. With intellectuals and industrial workers targeted, riots erupted in major cities, and Mao used the army to fight his own people.

Besides killing a lot of people—reportedly, between one and two million—the Cultural Revolution extinguished much of the country's history. Mao cited "old" institutions, from pre-revolutionary history to Buddhism to schools, as threats to the People's Republic. The Cultural Revolution made Mao's chairmanship into a cult of personality with the Red Guards, who had grown up under his rule and were loyal to him specifically. And anyone who wasn't loyal was either removed from the equation or forced to be quiet about it; it was a great risk to disagree with Mao. Mao's writings became required reading for all citizens, and his image seemingly appeared everywhere.

Mao remained chairman of the party up until his death. He did modernize the economy in some ways, most obviously in 1972, when American president Richard Nixon visited and the pair reopened relations and trade between their countries. Mao died on September 9, 1976, probably due to complications from Parkinson's disease, and his body remains on display in Beijing's Tiananmen Square. In an ironic statement, given how many lives and how much history his leadership had cost the country, the announcement of his death claimed that "all victories of the Chinese people were achieved under the leadership of Chairman Mao." •

NELSON MANDELA

THE TIME: *1918–2013*

THE PLACE: *South Africa*

THE OPPONENT: *Apartheid*

When Nelson Mandela began rebelling against South Africa's racist apartheid policies, even the most optimistic of supporters wouldn't have expected him to have such remarkable success. After his early rebellion led to nearly three decades in prison, he returned to become the first democratically elected leader of a desegregated South Africa, the architect of a new and diverse society, and an elder statesman honored worldwide for his commitment to peace and justice.

Born into the royal line of the Thembu tribe in 1918, Rolihlahla Dalibhunga Mandela was the first in his family to attend school (where he was given his Western-style first name), and then he briefly attended a regional university. After his father died when he was nine, Mandela was adopted by an influential local regent, who prepared him for a tribal leadership role.

However, Mandela instead moved to Johannesburg in 1941 to avoid an arranged marriage. There, he worked as a law clerk and attended law school as the University of the Witwatersrand's only native African student. He also joined the left-wing African National Congress political party, co-founding its youth league, the ANCYL. Where the ANC had been a fairly passive black-liberation organization, Mandela believed in active non-violent resistance and civil disobedience, and he turned the ANCYL into a more activist, grassroots movement.

Just a few years later, the discrimination and segregation black South Africans already faced under the law became even worse. The 1948 election went to a new National Party, which was dominated by Afrikaners and was openly racist in its platform. The party introduced the policy of apartheid, further dividing the country by race. Under apartheid, the government relocated thousands of

A POPULAR CAUSE

In the 1980s, Mandela's freedom became a popular cause far outside South Africa. In the realm of pop culture, supporters organized concerts to commemorate his seventieth birthday, and a coalition of famous musicians organized a boycott and refused to play in South Africa.

Mandela also brought together political rivals. He was so universally respected that, along with the 1993 Nobel Prize (given to him and F. W. de Klerk), he received both the United States Presidential Medal of Freedom and the Soviet Union's Order of Lenin.

people in order to segregate them, required non-whites (mostly blacks, but also Indians and people of mixed races) to register, and made political and financial discrimination official government policy.

Though a minority in terms of population, the Afrikaners had found a way to become even more dominant in terms of government. So, about a year after apartheid became official, the ANC adopted Mandela's plan to use active non-violence to fight for equality for all South Africans.

By 1952, Mandela had set up the first black law practice in South Africa to challenge apartheid laws, and that same year he got arrested for the first time for leading a protest. Apartheid policy included Pass Laws, which required black Africans to carry paper passes at all times, which white officials could demand to see. Mandela urged supporters not to comply with the law and burnt his own passbook in public, intentionally provoking an arrest.

As Mandela became a prominent leader, the government "banned" him several times, preventing him from speaking in public or associating with other banned anti-apartheid activists. In 1956, he was one of 156 anti-apartheid activists arrested and tried for treason (they weren't convicted, but it took years to resolve the case).

After a 1960 protest in Sharpeville—in which white police shot unarmed black demonstrators, killing sixty-nine and wounding nearly 200 more—the government declared the ANC an illegal organization and began arresting its members. Mandela had to go underground to avoid arrest or murder by the police. Though the government was trying to silence him, his success at staying hidden only made him more of a hero to many.

Though Mandela and the ANC had always advocated non-violence, he announced a change of heart while underground (saying that the ANC's strategy wasn't working) and prepared acts of anti-government sabotage. He became head of the organization's new military wing Umkhonto we Sizwe ("Spear of the Nation"), which set off bombs to sabotage government infrastructure and organized a disruptive three-day worker strike. Mandela then left the country for about six months, trying to raise support for the anti-apartheid cause and learning guerrilla tactics in Algeria for a possible action against government troops. After sneaking back into the country, he lived with other ANC leaders in the suburb of Rivonia, where they planned next steps.

However, Mandela was arrested at a roadblock on August 5, 1962. Because the police didn't have enough evidence to link him to the sabotage campaign, they charged him with leaving the country illegally and with inspiring the national strike. He was sentenced to five years in prison.

While he was incarcerated, however, South African authorities discovered and raided the Rivonia hideout. They found evidence of planned guerrilla operations against the apartheid government, arrested several of Mandela's ANC colleagues, and charged them (and Mandela) with sabotage and a conspiracy to overthrow the state violently.

The defendants admitted to the sabotage but denied planning violence, and Mandela gave a memorable defense of their actions in support of "a free society in which all persons will live together in harmony and with equal opportunities." They avoided the death penalty, but on June 12, 1964, Mandela and the other ANC leaders were convicted, sentenced to life in prison, and taken to high-security Robben Island off the coast of Cape Town. The revolutionaries endured hard labor in a rock quarry and were forbidden from speaking with one another.

Mandela would spend the next twenty-seven years in prison, eighteen of them in a tiny cell in Robben. His words and even photographs of him were banned by the government, which continued to pass even more apartheid laws. By 1970, black South Africans had lost all rights to vote, the right to representation in Parliament, and even their collective citizenship.

A young Nelson Mandela in 1937.

THE CHAMPIONSHIP

In 1995, South Africa was already scheduled to host the Rugby World Cup, and Mandela used the occasion as another way to heal the racial divide. By getting personally involved as the most visible fan of a team blacks had long rooted against and getting to know the players personally, he used the underdog Springboks' unlikely championship as something all South Africans could cheer together. And it worked. When he appeared on the field before the championship match wearing the Springboks team jersey, a sold-out (and mostly white) crowd chanted his name and gave him a standing ovation—a sight unthinkable just a few months earlier.

While Mandela remained in prison, a new generation took up the fight against apartheid. In 1976, students in Soweto carried out another uprising. The government killed hundreds, which drew international attention to what was happening, and the ANC exiles overseas began to organize more protests. Another round of revolution began in the 1980s, with the government again ordering a crackdown and giving security forces authority to kill and arrest huge numbers of protesters.

The ANC and Mandela's wife, Winnie, invoked his name throughout the struggle, and Mandela's freedom became an international cause to the point that the government considered releasing him as a symbolic gesture (and out of fear that his death in prison could cause the situation to explode even more). By 1988, Mandela was secretly moved to house arrest on the mainland, and government officials began to meet with him to negotiate his release if he renounced the ANC. Though some members of his party feared he was being manipulated, Mandela refused to abandon his stance that apartheid needed to end. When a new president, F. W. de Klerk, took office in 1989, he soon announced plans to release the man many whites still saw as a terrorist, but who had become a symbol of hope in absentia.

On February 11, 1990, Nelson Mandela finally became a free man. Huge crowds gathered to watch him walk out of prison.

Of course, Mandela returned to a South Africa still under apartheid. The year after his release, he was named president of the ANC and began to negotiate with de Klerk on a path to free elections. Still, Mandela's release didn't stop the chaos in the country, and interracial violence continued as the negotiations dragged on. In 1993, the assassination of an ANC leader brought the country close to civil war. Mandela made a televised speech calling for free and public elections as the only solution to ending the continuing violence.

In the 1994 elections, the majority of South Africans were allowed to vote for the first time and overwhelmingly supported Mandela and the ANC, which received more than 62 percent support in a multi-party election. On April 27, Mandela was elected South Africa's first black president—and the date is still celebrated nationwide as the public holiday Freedom Day.

Mandela would have had good cause to strike back against the country's former leaders, but instead he chose reconciliation. Promising to be a president for all South Africans, he put together a racially diverse coalition government (with de Klerk as deputy president), introduced social and economic laws to improve things for non-whites, and oversaw the creation of a new, apartheid-free constitution. Against all odds, he turned South Africa into a country with majority rule while maintaining minority rights.

Mandela could have served as president for life, but he chose to seek only one term and retired in 1999 at age eighty-one. He spent more than a decade as a private citizen activist, working on issues from racial and gender equality to AIDS awareness and international peace. A worldwide icon right to the end, Nelson Mandela died of a lung infection on December 5, 2013, at age ninety-five, in the free South Africa he helped create. ●

Malcolm X at a Martin Luther King press conference in 1964.

MALCOLM X

THE TIME: *1925–1965*

THE PLACE: *United States*

THE OPPONENT: *Racism*

The struggle for equal rights for African-Americans found a strong voice in Martin Luther King, Jr. Around the same time, however, Americans were introduced to another strong voice in the Nation of Islam's Malcolm X, whose ideas about black nationalism and separatism also gained a significant following.

The son of a Christian preacher who supported Marcus Garvey's Back to Africa movement, he was born Malcolm Little in 1925 in Omaha, Nebraska. His father's activism made him a target of white supremacists, and the senior Little received direct threats from the Black Legion, a splinter group of the Ku Klux Klan. The Little family moved to Michigan to escape the threats, but when Malcolm was six, his father was found dead. Though he was probably murdered by members of the secretive supremacist group, authorities at the time ruled it a suicide, denying survivor benefits for the family. Malcolm's mother was institutionalized after a nervous breakdown, and the children were split up into various foster homes.

Broke and orphaned, the young Malcolm turned to crime, making a living in New York City and then Boston as a drug dealer, pimp, and thief. In 1946, he was arrested for larceny and sentenced to state prison in Boston. While there, he got interested in the Nation of Islam—thanks in part to a visiting brother who had joined the religion—and became a convert.

Though the movement's founders based it on Islam and identified it accordingly, the Nation of Islam was a very different religion, preaching an alternate view of history based on racial theory and black nationalism. For example, the Nation taught that white people were "devils" created from the black race by a scientist—obviously an appealing idea for Little, given his childhood experience. At that point, he rejected his family name as a "slave name" and took the letter "X" as a placeholder for the African name taken away from his ancestors. While in prison, Malcolm also began mail correspondence with Elijah Muhammad, the leader of the Nation of Islam, who would soon give Malcolm X a national platform.

When Malcolm X was paroled in 1952, he traveled to Chicago to meet Muhammad, who was impressed with his acumen and gave him a great amount of responsibility. Within a year, twenty-eight-year-old Malcolm was named assistant minister of the Nation's temple in Detroit. Malcolm X founded the temple in Boston and served as its minister, then took on the higher-profile role of minister at the temple in Harlem. He also created a black Muslim newspaper called *Muhammad Speaks*, and reached more potential converts (and raised money) by assigning all men in the temple to sell the papers on the street.

Under his leadership, the Nation of Islam grew dramatically. He opened new temples around the country, turning four temples into forty-nine by the end of the 1950s. The organization didn't release membership numbers, but estimates suggest it may have grown from a few hundred members to tens of thousands in just a few years. Muhammad eventually named Malcolm X the official spokesman of the organization, formally making him the second-most-important leader in the Nation.

All this was happening at the same time the civil rights movement was becoming a real force in American politics. In many ways, Malcolm X became a counterpoint to Martin Luther King, Jr. (see page 221) and the popular movement King organized. Where King preached peaceful resistance, Malcolm X considered him a pawn of white Americans, calling him anything from a "chump" to an "Uncle Tom." He instead argued that "there's no such thing as a nonviolent revolution" and that African-Americans should use "any means necessary" to fight back. Where King fought for integration, the Nation of Islam wanted separation and an eventual return to Africa. Where King wanted his supporters to get full voting rights, the Nation specifically prevented its members from voting or getting involved in politics. (The two men would only meet once, in 1964 and for less than a minute; King, however, was consistently gracious in his comments about their disagreements).

Not long after he became a national figure, however, a divide developed between Malcolm X and the National of Islam. Muhammad suspended him from speaking for the organization in 1963, when Malcolm X reacted to the recent assassination of President John F. Kennedy by suggesting to a reporter that it was a case of "chickens coming home to roost." For his part, Malcolm X was dismayed to learn that Muhammad—who had set himself up as a paragon of Islam's virtues and enforced strict religious laws among members— had fathered several children out of wedlock with women he'd hired to serve as the Nation's secretaries.

Also, because the Nation of Islam rejected any attempts to join the larger civil rights movement or get involved in politics, Malcolm X began to see the Nation as an exercise in inaction, content to talk about change without doing much about it.

He officially left the organization on March 8, 1964. The following month, he delivered one of his most famous speeches, "The Bullet or the Ballot." He encouraged African-Americans to participate in elections—a big break with the Nation's position—with violence as an option if the government continued to deny African-Americans the same rights as all other Americans. As he put it, "If I die in the morning, I'll die saying one thing: the ballot or the bullet, the ballot or the bullet." The speech signified his break with the Nation, while making clear he still believed in black nationalism.

Malcolm X's views on race and religion changed even more after he participated in the Hajj, the Islamic pilgrimage to Mecca, Saudi Arabia. There, he formally converted from the Nation of Islam to Sunni Islam, which rejected the kinds of racial divisions taught by Elijah Muhammad. He adopted yet another name, rejecting Malcolm X in favor of el-Hajj Malik el-Shabazz.

Upon his return to the United States, he created new organizations that would combine some aspects of his old religion with a more inclusive civil rights mes-

X, RATED FILM

In 1992, Malcolm X inspired controversy again, when a feature film based on the posthumous autobiography was released. The film's production endured a series of problems. When Spike Lee was announced as its director, members of the Nation of Islam protested the choice with public rallies in New York. Lee also faced budget issues, needing donations from a range of prominent African-Americans—including Bill Cosby, Michael Jordan, and Oprah Winfrey—in order to finish his film. The movie, however, turned out to be a critical and commercial success, rekindling interest in its subject. Denzel Washington, who had previously played Malcolm X on stage, received an Oscar nomination for his performance. The movie also sparked a fashion trend, making black baseball caps with the letter "X" a popular early-1990s accessory.

A NATION DIVIDED

After Malcolm X broke with the Nation of Islam, his role as its spokesperson went to the former Louis X, who had taken the new name Louis Farrakhan. He spoke out against his former colleague when Malcolm X left the organization, making threats against him in print, and members of the slain leader's family blamed Farrakhan for inspiring the assassination. Malcolm X's widow, Betty, said as much in a 1994 television interview, and the next year one of Malcolm's daughters—who had witnessed the 1965 killing—was arrested for allegedly hiring a hitman to kill Farrakhan. The assassination never went through, and the controversial Farrakhan continued to serve as leader of the Nation.

sage. He founded a religious organization called Muslim Mosque, Inc., and a secular one named the Organization of Afro-American Unity. He apologized for many of the more extreme positions he had taken while a leader in the Nation and rejected its anti-white racism.

His conversion, however, made him dangerous enemies. Nation members sent him death threats, his car was bombed, and the Nation newspaper he founded ran cartoons and articles calling him a traitor and depicting his severed head with devil horns.

On February 21, 1965, he was scheduled to give a speech at New York's Audubon Ballroom. Before he could begin, three gunmen simultaneously stormed the stage, firing on and killing the former Malcolm X at the age of thirty-nine. All three shooters were members of the Nation of Islam, based in Newark, and all were convicted of the crime. Elijah Muhammad denied ordering the murder, but he did mention that his former protégé "got what he preached."

During the last few years of his life, Malcolm X spent a considerable amount of time being interviewed by author Alex Haley (best known for writing *Roots*). *The Autobiography of Malcolm X* was published shortly after his death, and the book has since sold millions of copies. The Black Power movement of the late 1960s, headed by groups like the Black Panthers and the Student Nonviolent Coordinating Committee, was heavily influenced by Malcolm X, while his martyrdom at the hands of his former colleagues drove many former members from the Nation of Islam toward less-extreme organizations. ●

FIDEL CASTRO

THE TIME: *1926–present (as of press time)*

THE PLACE: *Cuba*

THE OPPONENT: *Cuba's dictatorship*

Fidel Castro's career is rather unusual for that of a modern revolutionary, as Castro succeeded at overthrowing his country's government while he was still fairly young, then held power for nearly five decades before stepping down on his own terms. Though his leadership as head of state proved a mixed blessing, his success as a revolutionary leader was a real underdog achievement.

He was born August 13, 1926, in a Cuba where political unrest was already a common problem. In just the previous sixty years, the island had experienced two wars of independence, a transition to becoming a United States territory after the Spanish-American War, an American occupation, an election, and then nationwide protests about that election. In 1933, Sergeant Fulgencio Batista overthrew the government in a military coup, ruling for a decade before ceding power back to his predecessor.

While still a college student, Castro started joining revolutionary causes around the Americas, even joining an aborted attempt to overthrow Rafael Trujillo, the Dominican Republic's military dictator. Though Castro was hardly poor himself—his father was a wealthy landowner, and Castro graduated from law school at the University of Havana—he was drawn to Marxist revolutionary ideas because of the poverty and inequality he saw around him.

That was a common problem in 1950s Cuba. Batista had overthrown the government a second time in a 1952 coup, and governed with a brutal military junta. After this second coup, Batista became deeply corrupt—he was later found to have collected more than $300 million in bribes and kickbacks. Batista's anti-Marxist government was backed primarily by the United States and by business interests there. Not just "legitimate" ones, either; with Batista's support, the Mafia became a huge presence in the country, with infamous American gangster Meyer Lansky building casinos, hotels, brothels, and racetracks. And while big money flowed into Cuba, few of its citizens received the benefits.

Castro initially tried using his law-school education to fight the government and filed a suit against Batista for violating the Cuban constitution. When that failed, Castro decided armed rebellion was the only option.

Castro's first act of rebellion in Cuba didn't go according to plan. On July 16, 1953, he attempted an attack on the Moncada Barracks, leading 120 men against members of Batista's army stationed in Santiago de Cuba. But the army was ready for them. When Castro's men arrived, the army fired machine guns at the rebels and forced a retreat, and Batista's forces captured the survivors. Castro defended himself and others in court, arguing that a rebellion against an unconstitutional government couldn't be illegal.

Both Castro and his brother, Raul, were among those sentenced to fifteen years in prison, but they were released early and fled to Mexico to plot another attempt. There, Castro met Ernesto "Che" Guevara (see page 215), a leftist revolutionary who would become an important ally and Castro's second-in-command during the coming revolution.

They organized an invading force of eighty-two—named the 26th of July Movement, in memory of the barracks attack. Using an old yacht that took a week to get there, they returned to Cuba in 1956. Once again, Batista's forces were prepared, taking just two days to kill or arrest most of Castro's men. A handful of survivors—including the Castro brothers and Guevara—escaped to the Sierra Maestra Mountains.

In the mountains, the rebels gradually gained support from the

PLAY BALL

Another thing Castro revolutionized? The Cuban baseball program. A lifelong fan of the game, Castro promoted it as a source of national pride and developed an extremely competitive (though technically amateur, and therefore poorly paid) baseball league. Cuba's baseball team excelled at international competitions too, winning gold or silver in the first five Olympics that included baseball. However, Major League teams coveted Cuban players, offering salaries many times what they earned at home. So, through the years, dozens of top Cuban players defected to America, taking dangerous journeys in order to earn millions.

There's also a popular story about Castro himself playing in the minor leagues for the Washington Senators . . . but it's just an urban legend. He was, however, considered a very good high-school pitcher.

local population. Not only did they raid army outposts for supplies and carry out guerrilla attacks against Batista forces, but the rebels also took over and ran schools, hospitals, and factories. They eventually gained total control of the mountains, prompting Batista to try one major offensive move to wipe them out. In the summer of 1958, he sent an army of 10,000 against the Sierra Maestras, backed by bombers and naval vessels. Though horribly outnumbered, Castro and his supporters withstood the attack, and then launched a counteroffensive.

After nearly a year of guerrilla warfare, Batista fled to the Dominican Republic, and Castro—still just thirty-two years old—had won. At first, the new government was led by Prime Minister José Miró Cardona, but he resigned after about a month. Castro, who had continued serving as commander of the military in the new government, took over the prime minister role in February 1959. At the time, he described his platform for Cuba not as Communist but as supporting "representative democracy and social justice in a well-planned economy." Still, he ended up putting together the first Communist state in the Western Hemisphere.

As a ruler, Castro was a divisive figure from the beginning. He began the First Agrarian Reform, a land policy that limited how much land any individual could own, distributing parts of large estates to more than 200,000 peasants and making them new landowners. He dramatically increased the number of schools, roads, and other infrastructure, and guaranteed all Cubans full employment. Cuba's poor benefitted from the new policies, but thousands of members of the upper and middle classes fled the country, with Florida becoming a popular destination.

Because he also nationalized many businesses that had been owned by Americans and began to develop a relationship with the Soviet Union, the United States government grew deeply worried about having a Communist state just ninety miles off the coast of Florida.

American-Cuban relations deteriorated very badly in a short time. President Dwight Eisenhower cut off relations with Cuba in 1960 and created a trade embargo that lasted throughout Castro's regime. Before leaving office, Eisenhower also authorized an invasion to overthrow Castro, a plan that involved Cuban exiles living in the United States. So, on April 17, 1961, some 1,400 CIA-trained troops landed in Cuba at the Bay of Pigs, only to be easily defeated by Castro's forces, who took more than 1,200 invaders prisoner. Some were tried and executed, though Castro traded more than 1,100 back to the United States for more than $50 million worth of baby food and medical supplies.

In 1962, partly because he feared another invasion, Castro agreed to let the Soviet Union base nuclear missiles in Cuba. When the United States discovered

HARD TO KILL

According to Castro's former Secret Service head, the United States tried to assassinate him as many as 600 times, with the majority of those attempts under the administrations of Richard Nixon and Ronald Reagan. Even if that number seems high, Castro definitely survived lots of these threats, and some were deeply creative. Among the craziest examples? An explosive device in a conch shell at one of his favorite diving spots, a wet suit coated in deadly bacteria, and a poison pill hidden in a hotel milk shake. The CIA also tried proving how deadly smoking can be, trying an exploding cigar and a cigar filled with botulin as murder weapons.

the weapons, the ensuing Cuban Missile Crisis heightened tensions between the superpowers, who seriously contemplated a nuclear war before finally negotiating an end to the thirteen-day standoff.

Castro switched his title from prime minister to president in 1976, continuing to rule as a dictator. In the 1970s, he also increased his international role. Cuba routinely sent aid to Communist rebels in Africa and South America, and in 1979 it became a leader in the Non-Aligned Movement of nations declaring allegiance to neither the United States nor the Soviet Union.

At home, his revolutionary government achieved some of its goals while cracking down on opposition. Cuba's literacy rate consistently ranked among the best in the world, equally high for men and women, and its health-care system was similarly successful. However, economic development lagged considerably, and thousands of Castro's political opponents were arrested and persecuted. The economic liberalization and collapse of the Soviet Union during the 1980s also left Cuba without a major trade partner. By the 1990s, Castro had to allow some private enterprise in Cuba, though most of the economy remained Communistic.

After years of poor health, Castro stepped down in 2008 and placed his brother and deputy, Raul, in charge of the country. Though it tried repeatedly to depose him, the United States had elected nine presidents during Castro's time in office, and its embargo on Cuba continued after he resigned. In retirement, Castro continued to meet with foreign leaders and took on an elder-statesman role, hosting a visit by the pope and getting involved in peace talks between rival factions in Colombia's ongoing guerrilla war. •

CESAR CHAVEZ

THE TIME: *1927–1993*

THE PLACE: *United States*

THE OPPONENT: *Unfair labor practices*

By the time the labor movement reached its peak, it had made things better for most industrial workers by improving working conditions, safety, and employee pay. However, for decades many of those benefits remained out of the reach of farm workers, who had never unionized and were often poor immigrants, easily exploited by their employers. Their fight was the one Cesar Chavez chose to take up.

Cesar Chavez was born in 1927 in Yuma, Arizona, where his Mexican-American immigrant parents owned a small shop they would later lose during the Great Depression. Chavez was still a young boy when he got his first harsh lesson in how the rich could exploit working people. His father, Librado, was ripped off twice in a land deal. First, Librado agreed to clear a large plot of land in exchange for the deed to a smaller piece of property. He did the work, only to see the landowner renege on his part of the bargain and sell the land to another man. Librado was ripped off again when he got a bank loan to buy that same land, at a lawyer's suggestion—and the lawyer then took the land when the interest rates rose higher than the Chavez family could afford.

Desperate for work, the family moved from Arizona to California in 1938, constantly traveling around the state to wherever Librado could work as a migrant farm worker, picking fruit in fields. The wages were low, and the family was barely able to eke out a meager living. The constant uprooting meant Cesar Chavez went to nearly forty schools by the time he would have started high school.

However, after his father was injured in an accident, Chavez dropped out of school to work full-time in the fields and support the family so his mother wouldn't have to work. He had just finished eighth grade at the time, and he never got a chance to go back.

In theory, farm workers like his father should have benefitted from the National Industrial Recovery Act, passed in 1933 as part of the New Deal, President Franklin Roosevelt's response to the Great Depression. Among its many economy-stimulating provisions, the NIRA guaranteed workers the right to bargain collectively through a union. It even specifically prevented employers from using the then-popular "yellow-dog" contracts, which made employees agree not to join a union as a condition of getting the job.

But even though the wording of the law didn't include exceptions, the government was willing to make one for farm workers. Thanks to enough congressmen from farm-heavy districts, that exception *was* included in the National Labor Relations Act, another New Deal program that for years protected most other kinds of workers wanting to unionize. After World War II, the American middle class grew at record levels, largely because of unions. Farm workers, however, generally remained working class or even working poor.

Cesar Chavez got involved in fixing the problem when he was in his early twenties. After spending what he called the worst two years of his life working in the segregated navy, he moved back to the West Coast, got married, and relocated to a poor barrio in San Jose, California, where he worked the fields like he had as a teenager.

There, in 1952, Chavez began attending services with Father Donald McDonnell, a priest who made social justice and labor rights important parts of his sermons. McDonnell also helped Chavez get a job with the Community Service Organization, a grassroots group working to organize Latinos in California through things like voting drives and advocating anti-discrimination laws. Chavez spent most of the decade learning on the job about organizing. He became a devotee of the method of non-violence protest advocated by Mohandas Gandhi (see page 162), and would remain committed to peaceful protest his entire life. Chavez was

POSITIVE REINFORCEMENT

As a rallying cry to inspire farm workers during his 1972 hunger strike in Phoenix, Chavez popularized the phrase "*Sí se puede.*" The UFW continued to use it as a slogan, and the immigration-rights movement adopted it during its 2006 protests around the country. Though the UFW used the English translation of "Yes, it can be done," it could also be translated as "Yes we can." The 2008 presidential campaign of Barack Obama used that phrase as its slogan and used "*Sí se puede.*" for its outreach efforts to Latino voters.

a strict vegetarian on moral (and health) grounds, and prided himself on asking nothing of his supporters that he wasn't willing to do himself.

In 1962, Chavez shifted his focus specifically to farm workers, co-founding the National Farm Workers Association with his CSO colleague Dolores Huerta. Membership was slow to grow at first, but in 1965 the NFW got its chance. That September, members of a mostly Filipino union (the Agricultural Workers Organizing Committee) walked off the job in Delano, California, in a strike against the area grape growers, aimed at both the wine-grape and eating-grape businesses. The growers had tried dramatically cutting wages, and Chavez knew they would also try to use that strike to pit other groups of workers against the Filipinos in order to create ethnic divisions and find a group willing to work for less.

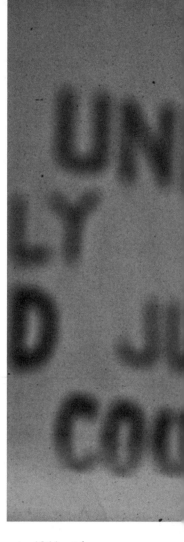

Before that could happen, Chavez organized his union to join the strike, insisting on solidarity among all the grape pickers. His organization united with the AWOC in 1966, creating what would become the United Farm Workers (the name it adopted a few years later). This would be the largest union of its kind in American history.

Under Chavez's leadership, striking pickers received national attention for their cause. Chavez led a march from Delano to California's capital, Sacramento, in 1966, with supporters marching about 340 miles to raise awareness. The union also pushed for a nationwide boycott of grapes, with members even going to grocery stores to educate consumers about the strike. As many as 13 million people eventually refused to eat grapes until the workers earned a fair wage.

At one point, Chavez refused to eat at all, starting a hunger strike in February 1968 that lasted twenty-five days. He lost about thirty-five pounds in the process. While it posed obvious health risks, the fast did get the word out about a strike that was already in its second year. When Chavez finally broke the fast, presidential candidate Robert F. Kennedy was among those who showed up to eat with him.

Chavez and his union scored a major victory when the Delano grape strike ended after nearly four years on July 29, 1970, and twenty-six growers signed

new contracts with the union. His ability to get outside support and use non-violent means made Chavez a hero, and not only to labor activists.

Though the Delano strike was his most notable achievement, Chavez had other reasons to fight.

In 1970, the UFW clashed with the Teamsters union over contracts to pick lettuce in the Salinas Valley of California. During a UFW-organized strike, the Teamsters swept in and negotiated below-market contracts with the lettuce growers. Some growers still chose to negotiate with the UFW, and the turf battle between the two unions turned violent. UFW members were attacked, a few were shot (two fatally), and a regional office was firebombed. Meanwhile,

A TIME TO REMEMBER

The early 2010s were a big time for the memory of Cesar Chavez. President Barack Obama proclaimed March 31 Cesar Chavez Day. He was unable to make it an official national holiday without Congress's support, but this act still gave the White House's stamp of approval to what was already a state holiday in California, Texas, and Colorado. The first feature film about his life, directed by Diego Luna and starring Michael Pena as Chavez, arrived in theaters around the country in March 2014. And in October 2012, the former UFW site where Chavez was buried was proclaimed a federal Cesar Chavez National Monument.

a court issued an injunction to stop the UFW from picketing, and Chavez spent more than two weeks in prison, arrested by federal marshals when he continued to picket.

The situation was a lot for the UFW to endure. Though its nonviolent tactics won the day, with the "salad bowl" strike ending in March 1971—and the Teamsters agreeing UFW had jurisdiction over farm workers—the deal ending the strike was still violated repeatedly for a few years.

Clashing with the Teamsters convinced Chavez that farm workers needed to get involved in politics as well as grassroots activism. His biggest success in that area came in 1975, when the newly elected governor, Jerry Brown, signed the California Agricultural Labor Relations Act. For the first time, an American state guaranteed in law that farm workers had the right to unionize and collectively bargain.

By the 1980s, with far more conservative governments taking over both in Sacramento and in Washington, the farm-worker movement struggled to get the state to enforce the CALRA. Chavez continued to fight for union rights, but he also expanded his activism to include protesting the use of pesticides, bringing attention to how they affected workers' health, and again organizing a grape boycott (as before, involving a hunger strike).

Chavez worked right up until the end of his life. He died in his sleep on April 23, 1993, at age sixty-six, in a hotel not far from where he grew up in Arizona. He was buried on the campus of the UFW's headquarters in Kern County, California. ●

CHE GUEVARA

THE TIME: *1928–1967*

THE PLACES: *Cuba, the Congo, Bolivia*

THE OPPONENT: *Dictatorships*

Though Marxist revolutions took place one at a time, Communist philosophy consistently argued for worldwide revolution. So, while most of the twentieth century's Communist revolutionaries—from Lenin to Castro to Ho—primarily focused on one country, Che Guevara got personally involved in a series of revolutions. It cost him his life, but cemented his legend.

Born in Argentina in 1928, Ernesto Guevara de la Serna grew up solidly middle class. Still, his family had supported the republican, anti-fascist cause in the 1930s Spanish Civil War, and encouraged his leftist politics. Even as a boy, Guevara had a wide range of interests and talents, including everything from rugby to chess to political philosophy. Like his future colleague Fidel Castro, Guevara was on track for a professional career before turning to revolution (though his track was medicine rather than law).

He enrolled in the University of Buenos Aires in 1948 as a medical student. However, in 1951, the twenty-three-year-old Guevara took a year off to travel South America with a friend (originally on a motorcycle, but it broke down along the way). Guevara credited that journey for his decision to devote his life to revolution, because it showed him the kind of widespread poverty South Americans lived with every day. He got to know and live among Chilean miners, indigenous farm workers in Peru, and even a leper colony in the Amazon rainforest (he used his medical training to help treat them).

Guevara's travels cemented his belief in pan-nationalism and in Marxist revolution as ways to improve life for the poor and working classes.

In 1953, the young revolutionary moved to Guatemala. The country had elected leftist president Jacobo Arbenz in 1950, and Guevara saw the president's land-reform program as an indicator that Guatemala was the kind of country he wanted to live in. Arbenz, however, was overthrown in 1954 as part of a coup supported by the CIA and the powerful United Fruit Company (which had claimed much of the land Arbenz nationalized). Guevara joined a militia movement to fight against the new CIA-installed dictator, but Arbenz gave up, fleeing the country and urging his supporters to follow suit.

Guevara needed the aid of the Argentine embassy to get safe passage out of Guatemala. The experience gave him a permanent nickname—"Che," a play on a popular greeting—and a permanent conviction that armed resistance was the only way for Marxist ideas to succeed.

He wound up in Mexico next, where he met Castro (see page 205), who was also licking his wounds after an unsuccessful uprising. They saw eye to eye right away—Guevara pledged himself to the cause the same night they met, after the pair spoke for hours. Castro knew Guevara's medical knowledge and intellect would make him valuable, and Guevara became a leader in the planned invasion of Cuba.

The face that launched a thousand T-shirts.

Guevara was among the eighty-two men who took a boat from Mexico to Cuba in 1956, only to be attacked and forced to flee to the Sierra Maestra Mountains. During the guerrilla war that followed, Guevara was an effective commander and strategist. He could be a disciplinarian, executing deserters and spies, but he also made a point of educating his troops and instructing them to teach villagers how to read and write.

He also understood the value of controlling the message. Guevara created a radio station in the mountains that could broadcast the rebels' message throughout Cuba. Still in use today, Radio Rebelde was an important tool for recruitment and for turning the public's existing dislike of Fulgencio Batista's military junta into growing support of Castro.

Compared to Castro, Guevara was often perceived as the more daring figure, more likely to try against-the-odds maneuvers. In one famous story, he ran into a battlefield without his weapon drawn in order to save a wounded soldier. During the revolutionaries' counteroffensive to take Havana, Guevara led his division on foot for a weeklong march to the capital, with peasants lining the roads to cheer their potential liberators.

In the final days of 1958, Guevara won a crucial battle at Santa Clara. Where most of the fighting up until then involved guerrilla tactics or small-scale skirmishes, this was a more traditional engagement, with fewer than 300 poorly armed rebels facing more than 2,500 garrisoned troops. Guevara overcame amazing odds thanks to his strategy—he divided his men into two columns to surround the defenders, captured (or possibly bribed government officers to acquire) an armored train full of weapons, and got enough support from locals who joined the fight. Santa Clara was the revolution's last major fight, as Batista fled the country after Guevara's impressive victory.

After the revolution, Castro gave his trusted deputy a number of important positions in the new Cuban government. One of those jobs put him in charge of the prison at La Cabana Fortress, where he ordered military tribunals and executions for a number of Batista officials considered war criminals by the new government. Guevara also ran Cuba's national bank, served as minister of industry, and led the agrarian-reform department, creating the blueprint for the country's post-revolution economy.

Where Castro was almost entirely focused on running Cuba, for the long term, Guevara saw himself as a revolutionary for other peoples as well. He often represented the Castro government internationally, speaking at the United Nations, negotiating for aid with the Soviet Union, and taking a multinational world tour.

In 1965, he quietly left Cuba, where he was still the government's second-most-prominent figure, and headed to the Congo. The former Belgian colony had become the independent Republic of the Congo in 1960 (today, it's the Democratic Republic of the Congo, also formerly Zaire). There, Guevara joined other Cuban and Soviet advisors aiding the Marxist Simba rebellion in the country's civil war, but this time the operation was doomed. Guevara—who kept diaries throughout his life—described his attempts at organizing guerrilla warfare there as a failure and saw the rebels as not truly committed to the fight. He stayed just nine months.

A FAMOUS FACE

Guevara's face remains instantly recognizable for a strangely capitalistic reason. On March 5, 1960, Alberto Korda—who would spend a decade as Fidel Castro's personal photographer—snapped a photo of Che at a memorial service for victims of a (probably CIA-organized) cargo-ship explosion. The image became iconic right away, and Korda allowed it to be used without royalties, figuring that spreading that picture of Che (which he named *Guerrillero Heroico*) could inspire revolution. Che's face became a popular poster design and a presence on T-shirts worn by millions. Korda did, however, try to prevent the image from being used in anything he thought Guevara would oppose. In 2000, he sued a vodka company for royalties after it used Che's image in an ad Korda felt denigrated Guevara's reputation.

He tried again on November 3, 1966, when he moved to Bolivia, sneaking into the country in disguise and under an alias. He brought only a few dozen Cuban supporters with him, planning to gain numbers by building support among Bolivian peasants. His guerrillas had early success against the Bolivian armed forces, but this revolution proved to be a disaster for Guevara.

CIA operatives had been monitoring him in the Congo and continued to do so in Bolivia, while also training the Bolivian military. While Guevara was convinced the public there would support him, the Bolivian government did all it could to undermine his support among the population, using both threats of violence and offers of massive financial rewards to get locals to reveal his whereabouts and betray his cause.

On October 8, 1967, Bolivian forces surrounded Che and his few remaining men in the village of La Higuera. In only about two hours, they killed or captured all the guerrillas—including Guevara, who had been shot repeatedly in the leg and had to surrender. He was executed the next day, along with the other prisoners. Even to the death, Guevara refused to sit for his killers, and his last words were reportedly, "Shoot, you are only going to kill a man."

More than one million Cubans turned out for a public memorial for Guevara, who continues to be a beloved figure in Cuba. Long after his death, schoolchildren still recite a daily chant promising to be like Che. When his remains were returned from Bolivia to Cuba in 1997, Castro lit an eternal flame at a huge public memorial built near Guevara's triumph at Santa Clara. For both friends and enemies, Guevara remains a powerful symbol of unbending revolutionary will, a complicated (but often inspiring) combination of philosophical guide and war leader. ●

MARTIN LUTHER KING, JR.

THE TIME: *1929–1968*

THE PLACE: *United States*

THE OPPONENT: *Racism*

Martin Luther King, Jr., grew up in an American South where, generations past the end of slavery, African-Americans were still second-class citizens under the law—denied access to the best schools and businesses, and facing huge obstacles even to vote. In a little more than a decade, it is fair to say that King and the movement he helped organize advanced civil rights further than anyone had all century to that point.

Born in Atlanta in 1929, King grew up in deeply segregated Georgia, which was then governed by "Jim Crow" laws. These laws created separate facilities for whites and African-Americans, from separate schools to separate sections at restaurants or stadiums to separate drinking fountains and swimming pools. King followed in his father's footsteps by becoming both an activist and a Baptist minister. After attending the historically black Morehouse College, he earned his PhD in theology from Boston University, making him a doctor as well as a reverend. While there, he met and married Coretta Scott, and the couple moved to her hometown of Montgomery, Alabama.

In 1954, King became pastor of Montgomery's Dexter Avenue Baptist Church, and he had moved back to the South just in time to see the issue of segregation finally challenged. That same year, when considering the case of *Brown v. Board of Education of Topeka*, the Supreme Court ruled against segregation and argued that "separate but equal" facilities were separate, but they were hardly equal.

Though it applied specifically to schools, the court had found segregation to be in violation of the Fourteenth Amendment to the Constitution and therefore

*Herman Hiller's 1964 photograph shows Martin Luther King, Jr.,
looking confident and assured — quite a feat, given the circumstances.*

MORE TO THE STORY

Under director J. Edgar Hoover, the FBI spied on Martin Luther King, Jr., constantly. Starting in 1963, the FBI bugged his home, his office, and hotels he visited, trying to prove (unsuccessfully) that he had Communist sympathies. The bureau also sent him anonymous threats—in one instance using details of an extramarital affair to urge King to kill himself or face public scandal (obviously, those tactics didn't work).

The FBI released some of its records on the King investigation in 1978, but the public won't get to know the full details about the surveillance of King for some time—a court sealed the full transcripts of the wiretaps until 2027.

illegal. And while Southern officials still tried to block school integration, the ruling gave the growing civil rights movement an opening to challenge segregation in general.

As one of the most segregated of states, Alabama was already becoming an important battleground in the fight for civil rights. In King, the pro-equality side would soon find the right leader.

The 1955 Montgomery Bus Boycott was the first prominent protest King helped lead, and its success proved that his style of non-violent resistance got results.

A local NAACP member, Rosa Parks, inspired the boycott on December 1, 1955, when she refused to give up her seat to a white rider and move to the back of a bus. Her protest got her arrested and fined, and the local NAACP chapter asked King—still new in the community but already considered an exciting presence—to head its planned boycott of the city's public transit.

King urged all African-Americans in the city to walk rather than ride on a segregated bus, and the vast majority participated in the boycott. In addition to facing the hardship of sometimes having to walk for hours to get to work, boycott supporters were often harassed, threatened, or even attacked (King's own house was bombed). The boycott lasted 381 days, accompanied by court battles, before the city finally agreed to desegregate its public transportation.

The boycott made King a national figure, and in 1957 he co-founded the Southern Christian Leadership Conference, joining a few dozen religious and civic leaders in an organization to promote non-violent protests throughout the South. King made sure that the fight for integration would always use peaceful tactics, both because he personally believed in them—he was strongly influenced by the success of Mohandas Gandhi (see page 160) as well as by Christian pacifism—and because he felt the American public would be more likely to support a non-violent movement.

NATIONAL HOLIDAY

King is one of few individuals celebrated and memorialized by a federal holiday in the United States. The first congressional bill calling for a federal holiday honoring King was introduced in 1979, but it failed in a close vote. The bill passed a few years later in 1983, and was signed by President Ronald Reagan—who had previously opposed it—after overwhelming congressional support.

Some individual states took longer, particularly in the South. Virginia originally combined King's birthday with Lee-Jackson Day, a holiday celebrating Confederate generals Robert E. Lee and Stonewall Jackson. That practice ended in 2000, with Lee-Jackson Day now held on a Friday and King's holiday the following Monday. That same year, South Carolina, the last holdout, made the day a state holiday.

The SCLC organized protests, marches and voter drives around the South, while King also traveled around the country and internationally to speak about civil rights and non-violence. Starting with Greensboro, North Carolina, in 1960, the SCLC supported a number of sit-ins, where black students would sit in the white sections of segregated lunch counters. Many were harassed, some violently, but more than two dozen counters desegregated because of their efforts. The various SCLC demonstrations often ended with members arrested—King was personally arrested twenty-nine times during civil rights protests—but their activism inspired others to join the ever-growing movement.

———

In 1963, King helped organize a series of protests in Birmingham, Alabama, one of the most segregated cities in America. The city issued injunctions against demonstrations in advance of the visit, making the planned protests illegal. King expected the police there, led by the firmly segregationist Eugene "Bull" Connor, to respond violently.

And they did, using attack dogs and high-pressure fire hoses against peaceful protesters. The news footage of such violence committed against marchers who didn't fight back, and were asking only for equal treatment, made a huge impression on the general public, and it was credited with winning over those who saw it. King was arrested again during the protests, and while incarcerated he wrote his "Letter from a Birmingham Jail"—an influential open letter to the American people that explained the need to violate unjust laws through peaceful civil disobedience.

Probably the most famous moment of King's career took place a few months later, when he led a coalition of civil rights groups in a March on Washington for Jobs and Freedom, bringing hundreds of thousands of protesters to the nation's capital. The march culminated in another of the seminal moments of

King's career: the "I Have a Dream" speech. Delivered August 28, 1963, on the steps of the Lincoln Memorial, King's address became one of the most famous speeches in history—a call for equality and a vision of a future where children would, as King put it, "not be judged by the color of their skin but by the content of their character."

———————

The civil rights struggle achieved one of its national goals when the 1964 Civil Rights Act overcame Southern opposition in the Senate and was signed by President Lyndon Johnson. The law banned segregation in all states, as well as discrimination on the basis of race, gender, or religion. Enforcement of the act would prove difficult at times, but the kind of Southern segregation King had spent his life fighting was finally outlawed. At age thirty-five, Martin Luther King, Jr., received the 1964 Nobel Peace Prize for his work.

The following year, Congress passed the Voting Rights Act, a law that made it illegal to discriminate against minority voters. Violence against SCLC-backed voting drives in Selma, Alabama, had demonstrated the need for such a law, and King had led a march from Selma to Montgomery to bring attention to the issue.

Though he's understandably remembered for those civil rights victories, King used his organizing skills for other important causes as well. He opposed the American military campaign in Vietnam and gave an influential "Beyond Vietnam" speech in 1967, linking the causes of peace at home and peace abroad. This harmed his working relationship with the White House, but King consistently spoke out against the war for the rest of his life. He also focused on the issue of poverty as a human-rights issue, organizing a Poor People's Campaign to unite anti-poverty activists and union members across the country and fight for economic justice.

On April 4, 1968, King was murdered in Memphis, Tennessee, when he was shot by white supremacist James Earl Ray while standing on a hotel balcony. News of his murder sparked riots throughout much of the country. King had been in Memphis in support of a sanitation strike, and had told workers just the day before his death, "I may not get there with you. But I want you to know tonight that we, as a people, will get to the promised land." •

JEFF FLEISCHER is a Chicago-based journalist and author, who has written for dozens of national and international publications including *Mother Jones*, the *Sydney Morning Herald*, *Mental Floss*, and *Chicago Magazine*.